Travel Sense

TRAVEL SENSE
by
Barbara Pletcher

Published in San Franciso by Harbor Publishing
Distributed by G. P. Putnam, New York

Travel Sense. Text copyright © 1980 by Barbara Pletcher.

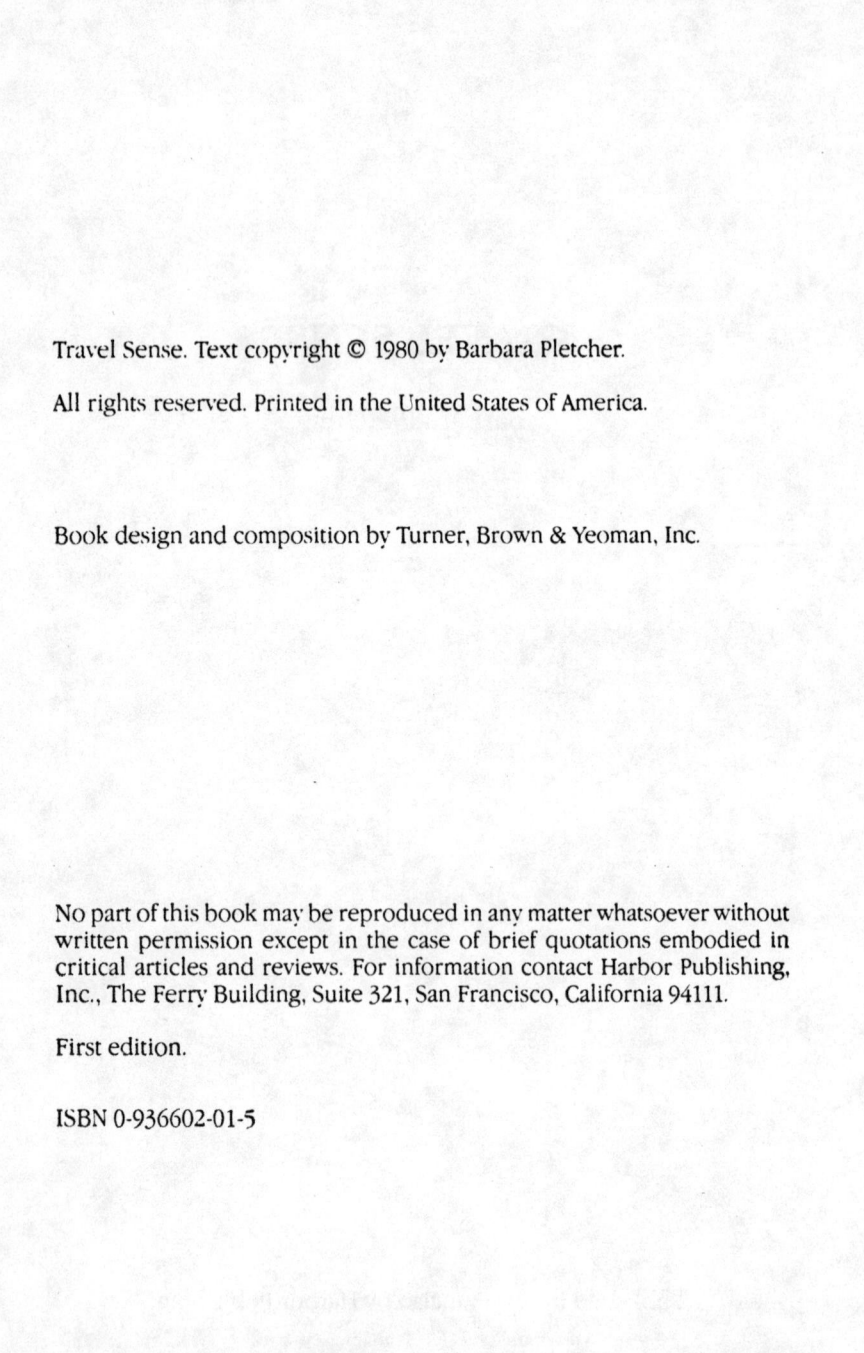

All rights reserved. Printed in the United States of America.

Book design and composition by Turner, Brown & Yeoman, Inc.

No part of this book may be reproduced in any matter whatsoever without written permission except in the case of brief quotations embodied in critical articles and reviews. For information contact Harbor Publishing, Inc., The Ferry Building, Suite 321, San Francisco, California 94111.

First edition.

ISBN 0-936602-01-5

Contents

1. Travel: Bonus or Burden   1
2. It's a Challenge, Not a Crisis   14
3. Getting Organized   44
4. From Point A to Point B   61
5. Your Home Away From Home   85
6. Thoughts for Food   102
7. Money Matters   118
8. Relaxation and Mental Health   136
9. Conferences and Other Special Destinations   146
10. The People You Leave Behind   171
11. Index   183

Chapter 1
Travel: Bonus or Burden

"We couldn't give that job to a woman. She couldn't handle the travel."
—Sales Manager

"Don't you think that your travel is hard on your husband and children?"
—Neighbor

"Why don't we save the company some money by sharing a room?"
—Male Co-worker

"Women are usually relegated to the tables near the restrooms or under the potted palm."
—Unhappy Female Traveler

Is business travel a bonus or a burden? Do women traveling for business and professional purposes automatically encounter travel-related problems? Why do these problems occur? Are women's travel experiences different from men's experiences? What can be done to avoid problems? Do the benefits outweigh the disadvantages?

All travelers encounter some difficulties. Women have experienced some special difficulties for two reasons. First, the number of professional female travelers has been increasing rapidly. Many of these women are relatively inexperienced. That in itself leads to some difficulties. Second, the business travel industry has evolved over a long period of time. For most of that history, business travelers have been men. The industry has been adjusting to women. It makes good business sense. But adjustments seldom occur fast enough to satisfy everyone involved. As more and more women see the potential in professional travel, the industry will make even greater efforts to satisfy the female segment of the professional travel market.

Fred Heckel, Vice President of Advertising for United Airlines, takes notice of some of the problems encountered by women while traveling and makes this observation:

> The problems we see women experiencing aren't any different from anyone else's problems. There are no special problems unless she makes them herself. And most of the time this happens not because of her gender, but because of lack of experience.

It is through increased understanding and intelligent decision making that you can more effectively handle the demands of professional travel. You will discover that it is both productive and satisfying.

Should You be Traveling?

Should you be traveling? Don't let anybody kid you. Regardless of the type of work you do, professional travel is important to your personal development and your career advancement. All of the people who make it to the top—indeed, all of the people who make it at any level—are people who travel. Business travel is essential if you're anybody, anybody at all. How can you be somebody and not be needed in more than one place? You may just want to be the proverbial big frog in a little pond. But, remember that big frogs often earn their titles because of some special knowledge or ability that they acquired outside the pond.

You may be facing opportunities to travel to conferences, company meetings, training sessions, or to meet with customers, government officials, or special interest groups. You may be considering a new position that will involve increased travel. You can look upon your professional travel responsibilities as a burden or a bonus. As with most things in life, what you get out of travel will depend on your expectations. If you view it as an intrusion on your life, as something to be tolerated, you will find that it will be just the burden you expect. If you approach it as an opportunity to grow and to expand your horizons, it will be a bonus. Whatever the purpose, grasp your opportunities and look upon travel as a bonus. Travel gives you the opportunity to build your image as a significant and successful person while you grow in self-confidence and self-determination.

> **Travel Gives You the Opportunity to Build Your Image as a Significant and Successful Person While You Grow in Self-Confidence and Self-Determination.**

You may be thinking, "I travel for pleasure. Doesn't that count?" Of course it counts, but it doesn't count as much. The difference is similar to the difference between volunteer work and paid employment. While there are many dedicated and hard working volunteers, volunteer work does not carry the same weight as paid employment. Pleasure travel says that you have the courage to challenge the unknown, but it lacks the credibility associated with accomplishing a mission. Pleasure travel is an activity in itself. Business travel is task-oriented.

If you work for a business corporation, travel says that you are important enough to be needed in more than one place. Your company is willing to invest big dollars in moving you from point A to point B. You are really needed. You are seen as having a commitment to your career. You can be trusted to take care of your business and to take care of yourself. It says these things to you, giving you just that little extra self esteem you may need to carry you through any of the attacks of self-doubt that intrude on all our lives. And it says all these things about you to all the people around you, thereby enhancing your success image. This person is important.

If you are in one of the professions such as education, medicine, accounting, journalism, engineering, politics, or law, travel allows you to develop professional contacts that add both to your knowledge and to your prestige. You have ranked yourself among the true professionals in your field. If you are in insurance, real estate, retailing, social work, government, banking, industrial sales, or in other people-to-people work, travel not only will help you build your people skills, but it will give you added credibility with your customers.

Some women find that travel is a requirement of their position. For others, travel is optional. Norma Bair is in the insurance business in York, Pennsylvania. A few years ago she attended a regional conference in Atlantic City of the National Association of Insurance Women. It was so rewarding that she went on to the national meeting in Miami. She met so many other women who had ambitions, interests, and concerns similar to her own that for several years she attended both the regional and the national meetings. As she continued to attend meetings, she made the effort to get more involved. First she was elected to the position of Regional Director. That only increased her travel responsibilities. Norma says:

> I learned to dislike waiting in airports and being tired from constantly attending meetings. These were, however, minor discomforts compared to the enjoyment I gained from this position, as I had the opportunities to meet with old friends and to make new ones. I had the chance to expand my knowledge and horizons to encompass a great many viewpoints in all lines of insurance. Further, if I hadn't learned anything in any of these conventions or seminars, I learned a great deal about the country and its beauties—and its not-so-beautiful areas. Another advantage has been building my self-image and my confidence in handling unfamiliar situations. I have confidence in my own abilities to handle whatever challenges I decide to accept.

Norma is now the National Education Chairman for the National Association of Insurance Women. Not only has she built a network of contacts nationwide and benefitted in terms of increased professional understanding and self-esteem, but her business has increased. It may be that her local customers are impressed with her accomplishments or it may simply be the result of her professional growth.

Learning to travel effectively and with confidence is an important part of your career advancement preparation as an upwardly mobile professional female. As your responsibilities increase, there is increased likelihood that you will be expected to be out of town for conventions, company meetings, or to work with clients. It comes with the territory. It is a test of your professionalism. Travel demonstrates your commitment to your organization and your profession. It advertises that you are willing to buy your job and its responsibilities 24 hours a day. It shows management that you have your personal life under control. It allows you to prove that you can meet challenges. You are able to put yourself in vulnerable positions and land on your feet.

Travel gives you continuing opportunities to grow in self-confidence, professionalism, and status. If you learn the techniques of efficient travel, you will be able to make the most of these opportunities. You will be comfortable and effective when you are away from home. You will be able to demonstrate to yourself and to others that you are a competent, confident, professional woman.

Travel Stimulates Self-Reliance and Decision Making

Successful travel builds your feeling of self-reliance and independence. You learn to depend on yourself and to trust your own judgment. Carole says that every time she is going on a trip she looks at her suitcase and does a mental take-off on Ed McMahon's routine with Johnny Carson. "EVERYTHING, EVERYTHING I could possibly need to get along on this trip is in that one little bag."

Joyce, an industrial chemist, remembers her first business trip. As she left the office, her boss's boss called after her, "If you have any problems, be sure to call me." She could only think, "What in the world is he going to do from 300 miles away?" And aside from that, most difficulties occur after office hours. She chuckled at the thought of awakening the pudgy little guy as he snored beside his wife. Later it occurred to her that he was only trying, consciously or unconsciously, to put her in her place. She knew her place and that wasn't dependence. She was determined that she would show him how well she could take care of herself.

Have you read any of the books or taken one of the courses on assertiveness? They usually include exercises and scripts with which you are supposed to practice being assertive. Role playing is great up to a point, but it's still role playing. Travel gives you a real live crash course. It's not a game: It's the real thing. After about the third time that you are literally left "holding the bag," you can automatically become very assertive. You may have acted out of desperation, but you still get to experience the fantastic high of finding out that it really works.

Travel Gives You A Real Life Crash Course.

For ten minutes Nancy waited outside the terminal at O'Hare for the hotel limousine. Then she watched passively as the driver swooped by at about 35 mph, busily engaged in a conversation with a passenger. Fifteen minutes later when he made his next pass, she was colder, hungrier, and even more tired. She was borderline desperate. She ran right out in the street waving her arms and yelling. He stopped. A few people watched the scene. So big deal. She got her ride. She would never have behaved like that back home in Ames, Iowa!

Travel accelerates your rate of new experiences. You've heard about the person who didn't really have 30 years of experience but had one year of experience repeated 30 times. Well, travel can give you the chance to pack 30 years of experience into one year. You can go back and forth to your work, back and forth to the same stores, movies, tennis courts, and people leading the average "rerun" life. We continue in those patterns because that's what's expected of us. We wear certain kinds of clothes and wouldn't be caught dead in particular stores or restaurants. "What would people say?" With travel you get a chance to encounter new situations daily. And you get to try out new solutions. We tend to get locked into certain patterns at home. When you are away from home, you are free to try new things. You can experiment.

Travel experiences give you lots of practice in making quick decisions and living with the consequences of those decisions. When you are in the protected home environment, it is easy to procrastinate. You can let those difficult decisions wait until tomorrow. If you wait long enough, someone else will make the decisions and assume the responsibilities for the outcomes. When you are traveling you are stripped of your normal support systems. You are forced to make decisions. You have to do something. You can't just sit down in the middle of the airport and wait for someone else to take care of you. You could starve to death. Professional travel provides exercise both in task orientation and in setting priorities. You learn to get the important things done first. Travel helps you to learn to accept that which can't be changed.

When You Are Traveling, You Are Stripped of Your Normal Support Systems. You Are Forced to Make Decisions.

A common criticism of women in business is that they haven't learned to roll with the punches. We are accused of being up-tight and inflexible. Travel requires flexibility. You have to conserve your energy. You soon learn not to get excited about things unless getting excited is going to do you some good. It really changes your perspectives.

As we mature, we move through stages. In a biological sense we distinguish the stages of childhood, prepubescence, adolescence, and adulthood. In a socio-feminist mode we might also distinguish four stages. The first stage is ignorance. Unfortunately, many women do not yet realize that they are entitled to all of the basic human rights. The second stage is inactive awareness when women realize that things should change, but lack the financial, physical, or psychological resources to make that happen. The third stage is defiance. Increased awareness and strength lead to counter-offensive behaviors. Women in this stage resent it when a man opens the door or offers to carry their bags. They become distraught at every misdirected comment. Third-stage women almost seem to look for opportunities to feel blows of discrimination. They're touchy. And people take advantage of that. It's a lot more fun to tease someone who can be counted on to react. Any older brother or sister can tell you that. Third-stage women are constantly out to prove their strengths and independence to others because they still need to prove it to themselves. Now they have done us all a great service in raising the consciousness of both men and women. Without the help of the women who have been visible in the third stage, we might all be stuck at inactive awareness. And we must all pass through the third stage in some way before we reach the next level.

The fourth stage is self-assurance. A woman in the forth stage thinks of herself as a person who can get things done and who happens to be female. She is comfortable with herself so she doesn't need to prove everything to everybody. This is closely related to her feelings of self-reliance and her ability to separate the important things from the unimportant things. If someone does something that is inappropriate, the fourth-stage woman recognizes that as the other person's inappropriate action, not as her personal shortcoming. Therefore she is less ego-involved. Rather than getting angry or feeling humiliated and carrying around the burden that rightfully belongs on the offender, she keeps things in perspective.

In fact, the self-assured woman tends to have fewer problems. She dispenses a certain aura of authenticity that delivers the message that she will take care of herself. You know that you have reached the fourth stage when you view an offender with the thought, "Gee, it's too bad that you're so ignorant. I'll just have to help you to realize that you shouldn't be treating me that way." Don't confuse self-assurance with complacency or lack of concern for the equal participation of women in any meaningful endeavor. It's just that self-assurance allows you to do constructive things without a loss of self-esteem. The goals are still the same; it's just a matter of focus and manner. Both stage-three and stage-four women create sparks, but the stage-three sparks are more likely to ignite controversies while the more controlled stage-four sparks can be more illuminating.

Business travel is the best substitute for the maturing experiences that men are assumed to have gained through military or sports activities. It gives women an opportunity to "earn their stripes." And, much like military service, travel experience has the added benefit of being easily communicated. As you move up in your profession you will be tested. It may be in job interviews or in annual appraisals. It may be in social encounters at cocktail parties or professional meetings. The underlying question is always the same. "Is this a professional person who can demonstrate both self-sufficiency and devotion to task? Is she really serious about her career?" Having professional travel experience is a big plus. Travel stories have at least as much interest and almost as much drama as war stories.

Travel Stimulates Professionalism

Travel stimulates your professional growth. The more people you meet, the better able you will be to make comparisons. You will be better able to judge your capacity and the quality of your work. You can elevate your horizons. And others outside your company will have the chance to see you in action.

Attending conventions and professional conferences gives you the opportunity to meet influential people in your field. Sometimes this helps you see how they manage to do what they do. At other times you will be amazed that a particular person has managed to do anything at all, and will realize that you have much more to offer. It helps you to get a better idea of what you can do. You're going to find that successful people are only human, just like you. But you must create your opportunities to participate and demonstrate your professionalism.

Maureen is a professor at a state college in Michigan. She had been tredding along doing her job well and being awarded the normal cost-of-living increases. One of her friends was working on a research project and asked her to join in. When the project resulted in a paper that was accepted at a professional meeting in Dallas, she decided she would attend the meeting. Her dean was less than enthusiastic and offered to pay for about one-third of the expenses. A meddling colleague urged her to skip the conference. He boasted that he never went to a conference unless he could make money on it.

Maureen discounted his advice. She dug into her own pocket to pay the balance of the expenses. After all, it's tax deductible. Since she was paying her own money, she resolved to get the most out of the trip. One of the things she did was to visit all of the publisher's displays. From that she not only got involved in some paid manuscript review work, but is now working on the teaching materials to accompany a major textbook in her field. She expects that the project will eventually provide her with about the equivalent of a year's salary, to say nothing of increased self-esteem. Her shortsighted colleague is still trying to figure out how to cheat the state out of nickels and dimes on expense money.

Travel also facilitates your professional growth in another area. As you move up the management ladder, it becomes more and more important to be able to delegate. In fact, failure to delegate is often cited as a management stumbling block. June Farrell coordinates the very successful seminar series, "Woman on the Go," for Eastern Airlines. As she puts it:

> Travel forces you to make the transition from worker to delegator because you're away so much that you have to trust subordinates to get the job done.

Travel Enhances Your Status

Most professional men manage to maintain and enjoy their status when they leave the office. At social functions, they are assumed to be professionals unless they clearly demonstrate otherwise—even if they are dressed in jeans. A woman is assumed less than professional almost in spite of her actions or dress. If she is dressed well, people think it is probably because her husband is successful. Even if a woman manages to casually bring her work into the conversation, it is often assumed that she has a low-status position. She must work for the attorney—she couldn't *be* the attorney! While you may be comfortable thinking of yourself as a professional, the vast majority of women are still clustered in nonprofessional work. It's just the law of averages working against us. It is as if your career status evaporates after 5:00.

Have you read the male-female class warfare literature that asserts that men are organized in a conspiracy to undermine and destroy the self-confidence and productivity of women? That's a pretty amazing thought. It gives men a lot of credit for coordinated action. The truth is that most people, male or female, are too busy worrying about themselves to spend too much time plotting for or against anyone else. Yes, there are some short-sighted, weak-ego males who consistently strike out against women. And there are some wellmeaning men who slip back into stereotypical behavior on occasion. But, as Eleanore Roosevelt said over 40 years ago, "No one can make you feel inferior without your consent."

One of the most significant factors contributing to the misunderstandings and miscommunications between men and women is the assumption of a lack of common experiences. When men avoid talking with women in public places or at social functions, it is often because they are afraid that they will get stuck with someone who is boring. There's only so much you can say about the weather. That's where travel can make an important difference. Just as fraternities have a secret word or a secret handshake, there is a commonality among professional travelers. A simple "When I was in New York on business last week..." can immediately establish your status as a professional. If you are listening to someone else's story and can drop in a comment on the city, the hotel, the restaurant, the airline, or the car rental, you are immediately an accepted part of the group, a first class person. Travel is a great equalizer.

> Just as Fraternities Have a Secret Word or a Secret Handshake, There Is a Commonality Among Professional Travelers.

So What Holds Us Back?

If travel plays such an important role in our professional development, why is it that the airports, hotels, restaurants, and rental car offices aren't filled with women? Why aren't there more traveling saleswomen? Why is it that men dominate the meetings of most professional associations and societies? What keeps women from seeking positions that require traveling and taking advantage of the many opportunities for personal growth and professional advancement?

Margaret was interviewing for a marketing research analyst position with a major appliance manufacturer. As a test of her self-confidence and dedication to her career, the department manager casually mentioned that the job would involve about 30 days of overnight travel each year. She cringed inside, having never experienced much beyond standard family vacations and an Easter break trip to Ft. Lauderdale during her college years. Besides, she had only been married a month and wasn't really sure how her husband would react. But she kept her composure and said, "Good, that will work out just fine."

After two years with the company, she moved on to another job, having never traveled further than downtown. Looking back on the situation, she figures that her employer used this technique to scare away the weak and nonassertive applicants. If she had responded, "Gee, I don't know if my husband would like that," she would have killed her chances of getting the job.

Fran has been with the same firm for 12 years. With a degree in accounting, a good image, and good people skills, she has managed to move up to the position of financial analyst within a very conservative industrial manufacturing company. But now she is stuck. Her manager knows that she hasn't traveled. In fact, she has a serious phobia about flying. The next step in her current career path requires that she call on the plant managers at the firm's outlying facilities. Cars and trains are out of the question. She will either have to learn to travel or she will have to define a different career path. She has enrolled in a course designed to help people with her problem.

Elizabeth hasn't even been given a chance to travel. Her manager has simply assumed that she isn't willing or able to leave her two young children at home and go off on a business trip. So everybody else in the office gets the out-of-town assignments and she sits at her desks and stagnates. But she has a plan to get around this barrier. She's going to invest the time, money, and energy to take a separate vacation this year. Her destination is New York City. She plans to seek out plenty of opportunities to talk about it both before and after her trip. If her boss won't take the risk of sending her on a trip, she'll do it on her own. It's an investment in her career.

Fear of Traveling   There are three types of fears associated with travel. First is the fear of physical harm. This fear applies to both business and pleasure travel. Some people are afraid of accidents, assaults, or drinking the water. Sure, travel exposes you to special situations. You could go out today be run over by a bread truck, too. But by learning the techniques of travel, you can minimize danger and be prepared to cope with whatever occurs. There is a lot you can do to provide for your own security.

Second is the fear of disrupting important personal relationships. This is far more significant with professional travel than with pleasure travel. You can schedule your vacation around your child's performance in the school play. You usually take loved ones with you on vacation. But business travel is scheduled around the task, not personal preference. How does travel affect the social life of the single woman? What happens to relationships between women and their husbands and children? If we wonder about a woman's capacity to balance a career and a family, we have to wonder twice about her ability to balance the demands of professional travel and the needs of her family. And there is that big issue of sex. Just the mention of travel is enough for evil thinkers to get that sly look and insinuate that your principle objective is to "fool around." If that's your intention, you don't have to go to the expense and inconvenience of travel. Just watch the soaps for proof!

Travel can disrupt personal relationships, but it can also strengthen those relationships. As you feel better about yourself, other people will feel better about you. If you're gone once in a while, you can become even more precious and exciting when you come home. Your friends and family will absorb a lot of your attitudes toward your travel. If you approach it positively, they will also.

If You're Gone Once in a While, You Can Become Even More Precious and Exciting When You Come Home.

But perhaps the most important fear is the fear of embarrassment. Travel is a kaleidoscope of new experiences, any one of which could be the source of discomfort or embarrassment. Staying home is security. Nothing ventured, nothing lost. Security is a tremendously strong motivator. The known and the familiar are comfortable—sometimes boring, but comfortable. The unknown is scarey. June Farrell points to some of the sources of this discomfort.

> Part of the uncertainty and awkwardness you sometimes feel when you're traveling stems from your being protected by fathers, husbands, and men friends who in the past have taken care of all of the mechanics of travel, entertainment, and dining out for you.

Kate Lloyd, Editor-in-Chief of *Working Woman* magazine, adds that women have historically been the keepers of the mores. We like to do things in the right way. When we're unfamiliar with what's expected of us, we tend to become uneasy.

You can look upon the unknown as an exciting challenge, or you can view it as a threat. Yes, you will end up in an unfamiliar restaurant and have to ask directions to the restroom. Yes, you will be talking with strangers. Yes, you may get lost. But you won't get bored.

Overcoming the Fear of Travel This book deals with each of these three factors. In the chapters on organization, transportation, accommodations, eating, money, and special destinations, you will find tons of practical tips and pointers on travel behaviors. You will benefit from the experience of other female travelers. The chapter on challenges goes through dozens of possible problems and inconveniences. It helps you with many precautionary measures to reduce your chances of encountering problems and also with practical solutions when problems occur. And finally, there is a chapter on how to deal with those left behind. How do you handle family, friends, children, co-workers, and everyone else affected by your travel?

This is a complete guide offering you the opportunity to hit the road at the same speed as an experienced traveler so that you can make the most of your opportunities. And the opportunities are there. Remember though, opportunities seldom knock. And even when they do, most people aren't ready for them.

If you want to get somewhere, you can't wait for opportunities to come to you. You have to make your own opportunities. You have to look for chances to go places and do things. In most cases people lack either the capacity or the interest to adequately judge your level of competence. They will evaluate you on the basis of their perceptions of *your* perceptions of your limits. If you say, "The sky is the limit," they're going to believe you."

Chapter 2
It's a Challenge, Not a Crisis

"If anything can go wrong, it will.
—Murphy's Law

Does Murphy's Law apply to travel? Why not? It seems to apply everywhere else. Here is a list of corollaries that should help you decide.
1. Nothing is ever as easy as it looks.
2. Everything takes longer than you expect.
3. If several things can go wrong, the one that will cause the most damage will be the one to go wrong.
4. Left to themselves, things tend to go from bad to worse.
5. Whenever you set out to do something, something else must be done first.
6. Every solution breeds a new problem.
7. Things go wrong in threes. If you encounter a fourth problem, it is not really a fourth problem, but the first of another series of three problems.

In *Living Hospitality* magazine, Management Editor DeWitt Coffman offered some substantiation for "Murphy's Law of Travel."

- Your plane always arrives at or departs from the gates farthest from the terminal.
- Whenever you get to the airport with plenty of time to spare, your flight has been delayed from one to two hours.

- Baggage checked in first comes out last. But if *you* check *your* baggage in last, it will come out — you guessed it — last.
- The "fasten your seatbelt" signs always come on while you are in the lavatory.
- In a 1000 room hotel, all 999 *other* TV sets work perfectly.
- All waiters and waitresses have 20/20 vision in all directions except yours.
- The hotel draperies close except for a half-inch slit through which the early morning sun drills a beam of light straight into your eyes.

One of the real advantages of travel is that it helps you to gain clearer perspective on life's little adventures. It gives you flexibility — the ability to adjust to situations. If you run up to the gate just as the jetliner is backing away, there is absolutely nothing you can do to bring it back. If you are due in Denver and you are stuck in Chicago because a blizzard has made the roads impassable, there is absolutely nothing you can do.

If you find that you have forgotten some important papers that you will need for a meeting on the next day, there is a lot you can do. You are faced with one of those golden opportunities to triumph over tragedy, to turn an obstacle into an opportunity. You can get on the phone and make sure that someone — even if it is the janitor — someone gets those papers over to the airport and into the "small package express — next flight out" system of one of the major carriers. And when those papers get to your destination city, you can have a messenger service meet the flight and deliver them to you at your meeting. It may cost you, but look at what you get. You now have the opportunity to impress others with your task orientation. You are making a statement: "This meeting is really important to me, so I went that extra mile to make things turn out as they should." You have saved the day. Of course, you want to gloss over the fact that it was your fault that the papers were left behind in the first place. But those things never seem to matter. If a basketball player misses five free throws but manages to hit the final winning basket as the buzzer sounds, that player is still credited with "winning the game." It doesn't matter that the five free throws missed earlier could have been the difference between winning and losing.

You soon learn to judge situations as controllable or uncontrollable. You learn to relax when there is nothing to do. Turn first to the telephone to make your apologies and then settle down. And you learn to act when there is something to do. You learn to depend on yourself and your judgement.

Some situations are important and others aren't. Some things just aren't worth getting excited about, but most folks get excited anyway and waste a lot of energy. Missing your flight is usually important. To find that the rental car company just gave out the last two-door and will have to send you off in a four-door for the same price is not important. It isn't even important if the hotel runs out of hot water. You'll survive. Cold showers are stimulating anyway. There are so many situations that can occur, you have to make these distinctions if you intend to keep your sanity. If you fret over every little disruption, you will end up with ulcers, and a nasty disposition.

If You Fret Over Every Little Disruption, You Will End Up With Ulcers, and a Nasty Disposition.

In this chapter, you will find lots of examples of important challenges that can arise on the road. Some of them pertain to your physical safety; others relate to your comfort and self-respect. For each situation you will find the precautions that can help you reduce your chances of becoming a victim, physical or psychological, as well as some suggestions on how to deal with the challenge, should it arise.

These are tested remedies. They have been recommended by experienced travelers as well as the people who provide the goods and services used by travelers. Now, don't be discouraged. It is better to know something about the challenges and be prepared than to be caught off guard.

Don't get paranoid. Murphy's Law need not apply. In fact, Murphy's Law is only a matter of selective perceptions. We pick and choose those things that we are going to notice, depending on what we are trying to prove or convince ourselves to do. Think about traffic tickets: If you get a ticket, you can chalk it up to Murphy's Law. You can even say, "Where are the police when I'm in trouble . . .?" But just think about all the times you speed, coast through a stop sign, or slip through on the orange/red light without getting a ticket. (I'm sure I'd owe the State of California thousands of dollars!) You can choose to count up the things that go right or the things that go wrong.

Crisis Conquering Attitudes

Before we get into specific situations, here are some general attitudes that will help you survive through and overcome any of the challenges you will encounter on the road. Your attitude can make all the difference.

A Positive Mental Attitude First, you must have a positive mental attitude, a *PMA*. Expect things to go right, and then work to make that happen. Most of life's events hang in the balance. When you expect something to go wrong, you can swing that balance against yourself. If you expect the best, people are often reluctant to disappoint you. And even if things do go wrong, you are at least happy until it hits you.

Expect Things to Go Right, and Then Work to Make That Happen.

Even when something does go wrong, you can keep your positive attitude. Keep saying to yourself, "There is a solution. This will work out. I may not know how right now, but I am confident that things will work out." Don't panic. Take a deep breath, reassure yourself, and then act. *Do something.*

An Action Attitude Couple your PMA with an *action attitude*. Remember, left to themselves, things tend to get worse. At home you can go to bed and hope things will be better in the morning or that someone else will take care of the situation for you. On the road, you are going to have to do something yourself. You can't hide out in your hotel room indefinitely. Would you rather leave your destiny to some stranger or take charge of yourself? Tell yourself, "I am going to do something. I'm going to do my best to correct this situation and I'm going to do it right now. I'll do what it takes and I'll deal with the consequences later."

I'll Do What It Takes and I'll Deal With the Consequences Later.

When interviewed on a talk show, a flight attendant who had survived a crash landing made an interesting statement.

> In a survivable crash, the people who make it out alive are the people who act fast — the ones who get up and get out of the

plane. The people who sit there waiting for someone to tell them what to do are the ones who are the most likely to become statistics.

Some people don't even act when they are told what to do. It is better to suffer the temporary embarrassment of hustling for the exit when someone shouts "FIRE!" than to sit there and be cool until you fry.

I was staying in the Omni Hotel in Norfolk, Virginia. I had gone to bed about 1:30 AM after washing and setting my hair. I was sleeping soundly when I became aware of a bell ringing. In my partial consciousness, I pounded on the night stand searching for my alarm clock. That didn't do any good. My next hazy thought was of the telephone, but by now my rational mind was saying, "Dummy, that's a constant ringing and the telephone is intermittent." I knocked the telephone on the floor anyway as the ringing continued. I finally awoke enough to realize that the sound was coming from the hall. I stumbled to the door wearing nothing but my curlers and clutching my sheet. Not acting too smart, I opened the door just as a man in a business suit ran by. It was a fire alarm. He was the night manager running to check out the situation.

Get Your Clothes On. We're Getting Out of Here!

A middle-aged woman opened the door across the hall. In a flash, she had me by the arm and was yelling, "Get your clothes on. We're getting out of here!" Still in a fog, I did just as she said. I pulled on my raincoat and grabbed my tray of 35mm slides. (Later I would realize how ridiculous that was. If the hotel burned down, there would be no conference at which to speak.) As she hustled me out to the parking lot, she explained that she had been in a house fire as a child and that we were going to be safe. Lots of people were standing around in the hallways and the lobby. They never did move their bodies out of the hotel. I stood in the rain in the parking lot with my cautious new acquaintance for almost an hour until the fire trucks left. It had been a false alarm.

But standing there in the rain was worth it, since I learned two things. First, hotel fire alarms are loud enough to wake the dead. That comforts me a great deal. Second, when you read about a hotel fire disaster, remember that there might well have been plenty of time to escape but people were too skeptical, too shy, too lethargic, or too dumb to take advantage of it. They didn't want to be embarrassed, so they waited until they saw the flames.

Now, I was pleased that I did something, but I can't help but think how foolish I was in the process. First, I should never have opened the door without feeling to see if it was hot. Second, I should never have opened the door without checking to see if there was someone there to pounce on me. Third, I should have put my raincoat on before I opened the door. And more importantly, I know that I might have been among the loiterers except for my neighbor. Now that I've thought about it, I'll be one of the first out of the building if I'm ever in that situation again.

Recounting my story to a friend led him to tell me of his experience with a real fire. He was on a business trip to San Jose. He heard a commotion in the hall and blamed it on "those lousy drunks." Then someone pounded on his door and yelled, "FIRE!" He stumbled into his pants and ran to rouse his colleague who had the next room. When he pounded and yelled, his friend responded, "Just a minute." He persisted, "Open the door, there's a fire." The other man finally opened the door and my friend got to see what had caused the delay. The hotel was really on fire and this man was packing his suitcase. People do crazy things in a crisis!

I Am Responsible for Me!

A Self-Determination Attitude The third important attitude is self-determination. Remember that you are the only one you can really count on in the end. You must look out for yourself. "I am responsible for me!" Don't sit there waiting for someone else to come up with a solution. Get up and ask questions. Don't accept second-hand information. Take care of yourself. You will find many helpful people along the way, but remember that others are looking out for their own best interest first, and in a lot of cases they don't even do that very well. Usually the best you can expect is a pitiful lack of interest.

Maxine had arrived in Chicago at about 7:00 PM. She hurried to check in at her hotel because she was already late to meet a friend for dinner. Her friend was staying at a nearby hotel. She walked over to that hotel only to find out there was no answer in his room. She went to the desk, gave her name, and asked if he had received her last message. The clerk looked in the message box and announced that there was no message from Maxine to

Bill. Since she knew he had gone sailing that day, she assumed that he had not yet returned. So she sat in the lobby and waited.

What the clerk didn't do was hand over the message from Bill to Maxine. When he had realized that they would be late for their dinner reservation, he had gone on ahead and left both the directions and the cab fare for her in a sealed envelop. Had Maxine persisted and asked if there was a message for her, the evening might have been saved. It wasn't. The clerk could have cared less.

Full Utilization of the Available Resources

Once you have the proper attitude, the next step is to gather your resources. Immediately ask yourself, "What resources do I have to work with? Who can help me?" In the spring of 1979, heavy rains caused flooding in the streets of Houston. Having finished up an evening meeting in the Shamrock Hilton Hotel, I was about to head for a flight on Texas International Airlines out of Hobby Field, the close-in intra-Texas airport. I had an important early morning appointment in Dallas.

Then the lights went out. With a candle from the dining room, I managed to call the airport and establish that the planes were still taking off. I was encouraged. Having managed to balance the candle, telephone book, and dime and having dialed without setting myself on fire had to be a good sign. Now, the only trick was to get to the airport. The airport limo was parked in front of the hotel, but the driver wasn't moving. Cabs were out of the question. An Air France flight crew bus was there, but even a "down-on-one-knee" routine did little good. They were bound for the international airport, but it had been shut down by the weather. The French crew was going to check back into the hotel. There were no rental cars available at the hotel.

I went back to the banquet to look for someone to help. I found a local person who had a car. Jim Nicholson from DatagraphiX Corporation had been one of the exhibitors at the trade show part of the meeting. With a sense of adventure, he tried four or five routes and finally got through the flooded streets and lines of stalled cars to deliver me to the airport. I had made use of the resources available.

Post-crisis behavior is important, too. Beware of the "Monday Morning Quarterbackers." You may have suffered through a situation only to get back to the office where somebody pontificates,

"Gee, why didn't you . . ." or "If I had been there I would have . . ." Your own mental health and self-esteem require reminding yourself that you did the best you could with the situation as you saw it and the resources available to you at that moment. These smart-mouths are sitting in a perfectly calm setting with no risk and lots of time to think about it. They weren't there. There is no way of telling how well they would have handled it had they been there —regardless of their claims. Of course, it's always fair to ask yourself, "What can I learn from this?"

Three Powers to Cope With Challenges

Here are some general techniques that have been proven effective in a variety of crises. They will work at home as well as on the road. All they require are a healthy dose of self-esteem and a measure of self-control.

The Power of Silence Juanita was on her way to check in for an American Airlines flight at Boston's Logan airport. An experienced traveler, she looked up to find that she had been wasting time standing at the counter clearly labeled "Small Package Express Service" instead of the baggage check-in. The reason was that she had been distracted by a commotion in another line. It seems that a young man who had intended to take a flight for Chicago with a scheduled departure of 7:45 PM had arrived at the gate at 7:45 PM+ as the plane was being towed out to the runway. While it was his watch against the airline's clock, he was proceeding to make the situation worse.

He was in an absolute rage and was venting it all on the ticket agent. Now the ticket agent had not caused the young man to miss his plane. But airline employees are well trained. The ticket agent was patiently explaining the airline regulations on boarding times and responsibilities. The plane was gone. That wasn't going to change. This young man, in his lack of experience, was alienating the one person who could do him the most good, and he was making a fool of himself in the process.

He should have used the *Power of Silence*. The world is full of gatekeepers—people like the teller who can approve your check, the librarian who can check out your books, and the salesclerk who can check in the stockroom. These people have a variety of little things they can do to make your life more pleasant or to close you out. That airline ticket agent has a computer terminal.

For a cooperative would-be passenger, she can immediately check for the next available departure on her own or another airline. But remember, you can't see what appears on her computer screen. She could stare right at an available seat and say, "I'm sorry, there is nothing available for the rest of the day." We know that she wouldn't do that, but she could.

The key to the Power of Silence is to realize that this gatekeeper has more potential solutions to your problem than you do. If you start ticking off your ideas of possible solutions—"Could I get on another flight?" "No, there is nothing available." "Can I connect through another city?" "Sure, but I will have to charge you $50.00 extra," and so on—you will soon run out of solutions. And you'll probably miss the best one. Beyond that, the gatekeeper holds all the cards. He or she can decide whether or not to pull strings for you. In a lot of situations you can't pull your own strings.

If you have a fit, the gatekeeper will quietly have the last word. It can be a lesson to others who might be thinking about being abusive to get their way. If you give up and go away, the gatekeeper will turn to other business. If you just stand there looking pleasant and expectant, waiting for the gatekeeper to come up with a solution, you will increase your chances of success. Smile and repeat the magic words, "Surely there's something we can do." Gatekeepers will begin to run through their mental files of possible solutions and pick the one which is most likely to get you out of the way. The Power of Silence goes hand in hand with the *Power of Joint Commitment*.

The Power of Joint Commitment If we stay with the same example, we can agree that it was the young man who had the problem. He missed his plane. The agent didn't have any problem. She was going to work for a few more hours and then go home. But had the young man been smart, he could have shared a little of his problem with the agent.

By saying, "Oh dear, what are *we* going to do now?" he could have pulled the gatekeeper/agent into the problem with him. He could have established joint commitment to the solution of the difficulty. He could have added an important person to his team. But, with the way he handled it, Juanita figures this man may still be wandering through Logan Airport.

The Power of the Telephone Think of it. There are little wires, optic fibers, and satellites that connect your telephone to every home, business, and telephone booth in the nation—or in the world for that matter. With just a couple of dimes you can do amazing things. You can direct dial 74 different countries, some with names you can't even pronounce. If you can do that, you can surely call and ask them to hold your hotel reservation even if it wasn't guaranteed. You can save someone from an aggravating pointless trip to pick you up at the airport when you aren't going to arrive. You can rearrange appointments. You can have duplicates of important papers sent off. You can get a telephone number or an address if you forget where you're going. You can even trace lost items. People hate to wait and wonder. If you are delayed, a phone call can make the difference between an angry reception and sympathetic assistance.

What Others Have Learned

You would have to be very creative to come up with a new challenge. We are almost always facing challenges which someone else has already experienced. Maybe they handled it well the first time. It's more likely that they learned by trial and error. Here are some of the challenges others have been working on for a long time. As Charles Moore, the author of *The Career Game*, puts it, "Life is too short to make all the mistakes yourself."

Blizzards, Storms, and Delays Regardless of your careful plans, you are still at the mercy of Mother Nature. Every area of the country has its special version of bad weather. Blizzards, tornados, hurricanes, fog, floods and other "Acts of God" can leave you stranded. Other than staying home most of the winter, spring, summer, and fall, what are some precautions you can take?

If you are traveling by air during bad weather periods, it can pay to keep up on the weather reports. It is often difficult to keep up on the news while traveling, but that will go on without you anyway. The weather reports are a necessity. If things look really bad, check before you head for the airport. And remember, most flights start someplace else and make a circuit. It could pay to check on the origination point of your flight. The flight itineraries are listed in the front of the Official Airline Guide *(OAG)*. It is better to be stranded at your hotel than to be stuck in an airport with thousands of people.

Summer can be just as bad as winter. Elayne was to leave

Detroit at 5:30 PM on her way to a convention in Minneapolis. She was to arrive at 8:00 PM and meet friends for dinner at 9:00. When the plane hadn't left Detroit by 6:15, she used the *Power of the Telephone*. Her friends assured her that they didn't mind waiting. That was the last they heard from Elayne that night.

The DC10 took off from Detroit at 6:45 PM for the one-hour flight to Chicago, where she was to switch planes to continue on to Minneapolis. It circled O'Hare for four hours before it returned to Detroit for refueling. The rainstorms in Chicago were still too severe and the airport remained closed. They sat on the ground in Detroit for over an hour. Since O'Hare might open at any minute, they weren't allowed off the plane without risking their rights to reboard.

Elayne was stuck. What was she supposed to do? First, it was impossible to contact her friends in Minneapolis. At least she had called when she had the chance to warn them of possible delays. This points out an important practice. It is better to call and say, "I don't know how this is going to work out, but be aware that I'm having a problem," than to wait until you can give the details. You may not get that chance to call back.

There Must Be Some Reason Why This is Happening to Me.

Elayne is a positive person, so she said to herself, "Something good must come out of this. There must be some reason why this is happening to me." She set out to turn tragedy into triumph. Elayne is in the public relations business and is always anxious to meet potential clients or to learn from other business people. The DC10 is a big plane. How was she to screen the passengers to see who would be a worthwhile person to talk with during the enforced delay? She reasoned that her prospect would be an experienced traveler and would therefore know enough to be carrying a pocket *OAG*. She started from the back of the plane glancing under seats; when she found briefcases, she stopped and asked the occupant if he or she had an *OAG*. When she finally found one, she started up a conversation about her business and passed the hours swapping stories and information with a sales manager for an electronics firm. And how does this story end? The plane finally landed in Chicago at 12:45 AM. Elayne didn't get to Minneapolis til 9:30 the next morning. That's really too late for dinner!

I've missed dinner, too. In this case, it was a picnic at home. I was having my son's undefeated little league baseball team over for an end-of-the-season pizza and swimming party after the last game. I knew it was going to be close. I was scheduled to touch down in Sacramento at 7:18 PM and figured that the team would touch down at my house about 8:15. I arrived at the Vancouver airport at 3:00 PM—a full hour early because of customs requirements. I settled back as the plane backed away from the gate, but sat up straight as the plane pulled back up to the gate. It seems it was having trouble with its hydraulic system. I am quite happy to go along with any pilot who believes that the plane is not airworthy. I am constantly amazed when people complain that the plane isn't taking off due to fog. The pilot has my proxy.

After being held on the plane for a half-hour, we were deboarded to wait in a room for another hour. When it was finally decided that the plane couldn't be fixed in a reasonable length of time, we were released to change our plans with the option of flying out on a different plane at 11:00 PM.

I headed back to the ticket agent and was first in line to pick up the $7.00 meal credit and book a seat on the 11:00 PM flight. That meant I would have to stay over in Seattle and take the morning flight into Sacramento. The airline agent promised that the airline would be arranging for rooms in Seattle. I asked another woman to join me for dinner, but first called home to confess that I couldn't make it and wish to my husband and son a good time.

When my guilt attack subsided, I went to dinner. The restaurant had large windows facing west and the air conditioning was on the blink. Dozens of people were sitting there cooking in the sun. That didn't seem too promising to me, so I scouted around and found there was a hotel only a $2.50 cab ride down the street. I organized a party of five fellow passengers and we all went to the hotel's lounge to relax. There was a woman named Billie Williams from the Baylor Medical School in Houston, a forester named Ed from Montana, and a couple of Canadian energy researchers.

We took turns calling the ticket agent in case there was any change. The 11:00 pm plane was going to be an hour late, but we got back to the airport just in case that was an over-estimate. I again checked with the agent who again assured me that rooms would be waiting in Seattle. Billie was getting concerned because she had to make a connection to Portland or else miss out on her first chance to see her new granddaughter.

By the time we got to Seattle, Billie's connection was in jeopardy, so Ed the forester volunteered to shepherd Billie's bags through customs and check them onto a plane for Houston. She could just hustle off to make her little half-day side trip to Portland. People can be very helpful if you let them know you need help.

My assignment was to seek out the airline agent and check on the rooms. Surprise! The agent asked my name and then informed me that they were only able to find three rooms and my name wasn't on the list. Standing there in a navy blue skirted suit and carrying a briefcase, I resorted to the Powers of Silence and Joint Commitment and asked, "Well, what are we going to do?" Having twice been assured there would be rooms courtesy of the airline, I really did feel that I had some right to ask. The agent wasn't cooperating and replied, "I guess you can sit here in the airport til morning." That was just too much at 1:30 in the morning.

Now, in most airline situations, it's best to ask for the customer service representative. This person is usually in plain clothes and has more authority than the ticket agent to act on your behalf. I didn't do that. I continued, "That just isn't going to do." He thought for a minute and then offered to let me stay in the little conference room behind the ticket counter. "There's a couch in there and you can at least lock the door."

Just about this time, Ed the forester reappeared asking what was happening about the rooms. I explained and offered, "Look, if there's only one couch, I get it. But if you'd care to spend what's left of this night some place other than the lobby, I don't mind." So I spent the night fully clothed in the little room behind the ticket counter with Ed the forester from Montana. In the morning we went our separate ways. I don't know what Ed did, but when I got back to my office I wrote to the airline explaining the situation and stating that I thought a fair settlement would be a refund of half of the one-way fare. The check and an apology arrived within a week.

> So I Spent the Night Fully Clothed in the Little Room Behind the Ticket Counter With Ed the Forester From Montana.

Missed Flights Everybody is going to miss a flight someday. This can happen even if you try to leave plenty of time. Joyce thought she had left plenty of time to get from downtown Chicago to O'Hare but had not figured on key streets being closed off for the St. Patrick's Day parade. Bonnie's travel agent switched over to a computer system. While the old itinerary had only listed departure times, the new one had added a column of arrival times. She had checked it twice, but misread the arrival time for the departure time. Bonnie arrived at the airport in time to catch a plane that had long since departed for her intended destination.

For several days it had been foggy all over northern California. When I started for the airport, I was expecting delays. I wasn't planning to check any luggage but glanced at the Hughes AirWest arrival/departure board at the counter on my way by. A red flag reading "delayed" caught my eye and confirmed my expectation that my plane would be almost two hours late. So I settled into a phone booth in the lobby and started making phone calls. Halfway through one conversation, I glanced toward the desk and got a sick feeling when I realized that the red flag was on the "arrival" half of the board—not the departure half. I was headed *for* Phoenix and the delayed plane was arriving *from* Phoenix. I hustled down to the gate just in time to board, but it was close and I felt like kicking myself for being so dense. I had expected the worst and had almost caused it to happen.

Mary checked her ticket carefully and arrived at the airport with plenty of time to spare. But when she handed the agent her ticket, he just laughed at her. She was booked for PSA flight 87 from Sacramento to Long Beach, California. However, that flight had been discontinued several months earlier. The travel agent had used an outdated *OAG*.

Remember Elayne and her challenges in getting to Minneapolis? Well, her troubles weren't over. She had been wait-listed on her return flight. She called the airline on Monday and checked to see if it had cleared. They said it had. But when she got to the airport on Wednesday, the agent couldn't find her name on the passenger list. The mystery was solved when a closer look at the ticket revealed that she was 24 hours late. She had been booked for a flight on August 7 and it was now August 8.

On another trip, Becky rented a car from an off-the-airport-grounds car rental company in Dallas. Its facilities were located in the hangars of the old abandoned Greater Southwest Airport next to shiney new DFW airport. On the trip to pick up the car, the van driver had cut off the freeway and driven across the old runways to reach the rental car office. When Becky returned to the airport on Saturday, she tried the same stunt only to run into a complete blockade of old tires and roadblocks. It seems that the local racing clubs hold races on those runways on Saturdays. She could see the hangar, but she couldn't get to it. She tried one dirt road only to reach a dead end. Frustrated, she stopped the car and started toward the barriers. This really got the attention of the race officials, who thought she was going to get killed on their raceway. They probably didn't care too much about her, but it would have delayed the race. They came running over and gave her directions to get to the hangar. With the tangle of freeways surrounding DFW, she had to drive about ten miles to get to the hangar which couldn't have been more than 300 yards as the crow flies. She had allowed an extra 30 minutes to turn in the car. She made it to the airport as the plane was boarding.

How can you avoid these challenges? The ultimate salvation is to live in a major city and travel only to other major cities. If you are on the Chicago—New York—Washington circuit, you have no problems. Planes leave every hour. If you are late for one, you're just a bit early for the next. If service to your destination is less frequent, leave yourself plenty of time, more time than you ever think you'll need. Ask your local contact or the hotel people for an estimate of the time needed to get to the airport and then add at least 30 minutes. It's far better to be early. Planes don't wait. Join the airline club of the airline you use most often, and look upon this extra time as an opportunity to make use of its facilities. It's not a waste of time. You'll get to meet other serious travelers and learn from their experiences.

Airports are becoming increasingly burdened. Some pseudo-macho travelers brag about their ability to cut their waiting time to the last minute. They rush up and run on the plane. It's not worth the risk. And besides, your heart is thumping so loud that you can't hear the safety lecture. The best policy is to move your body to the next required point as soon as possible. If the choice is between having a second cup of coffee in the hotel or going out to the airport and drinking your coffee there, get your body out to the airport.

Check carefully both on yourself and your travel agent. Check dates and check times. Then check again. Have faith in your travel agent, but check again anyway. Learn to mention days and dates each time you check your reservations. "Now that's 4 PM on Monday the 23rd of March, right?" Invest in the pocket *OAG* and keep it handy to check yourself out. It's worth the money if it saves you just once each year. You'll find the address and telephone number on page 69.

Lost Tickets People are amazingly casual with their airline tickets. They don't seem to realize that tickets are almost like cash. Someone can take your ticket to the counter and cash it in. In fact, there are organized rings of ticket snatchers. When traveling in foreign countries, you must also protect your passport. These are not easily replaceable documents. You can be in serious trouble. Treat your travel documents with at least as much respect as cash.

Treat Your Travel Documents With at Least as Much Respect as Cash.

Mary reports that she was traveling to the annual sales meeting with her sales manager. Because he was responsible for part of the program, he had several pieces of luggage. She was embarrassed for him as he stood in the airport lobby searching for his ticket. He searched his pockets, his briefcase, his sample case, the pockets of his suits in his garment bag, and on and on. There he was displaying all of his possessions to all of the passers-by and swearing that he had never lost a ticket in 15 years of travel. He must have been very lucky.

The logical precaution is to treat your ticket with respect. Never leave your ticket in your room. Carry it with your money. To avoid losing your ticket, you should have a special place for it and always keep it there. It may be a pocket in your briefcase or a flap in your pocket calendar. It's also a good idea to have a copy of your itinerary tucked away someplace else so that you can at least reconstruct it if you lose the ticket. Immediately upon boarding the plane, take the time to return your ticket to its accustomed place. Some people do foolish things like tucking their ticket in the seat pocket in front of them. Two hours later they leave both the plane and their ticket.

If you have lost your ticket, you are going to have to buy a new one. Your old reservation will still be there, but you are going to have to come up with the price of the ticket. And if you had purchased the first ticket with a discount, you may even have to pay full fare this time. This is where charge cards are important. It isn't always easy to come up with $300 in cash on a moment's notice.

An American Express card may be important if the ticket is an expensive one. Unlike the bank cards, American Express has no credit limit. You may not be able to clear the price of the second ticket on your bank card. If you don't have either the cards or the money, as might be the case if you lost your purse or briefcase, you can cover yourself if you can call back to your home or office and get someone to buy you a ticket at that end. You can pick that ticket up at your end as a prepaid ticket.

If you know where you lost your ticket, you are in pretty good shape. Sarah was at a meeting in Raleigh, North Carolina. Her ticket wouldn't fit in her evening bag so she dropped it in the desk in the hotel room and said to herself, "Now don't forget that in the morning." When she got to the airport at 6:00 AM to catch the first flight for her trip to the West Coast, she realized her error. But it was too late. While changing planes in Washington, she called the hotel and explained. They mailed her the ticket and she turned it in for a refund.

If you have really lost your ticket, you have to buy a new ticket and fill out a lost ticket form. If the ticket is not used within about six months, the airline assumes it has been destroyed and sends a refund less a $5.00 service charge. Your money is tied up all that time. But if someone uses the ticket, you are liable. You bought someone a plane ride.

Belongings Left on the Plane One of the flight attendant's responsibilities is to welcome you to the arrival city, give you the time of day, and caution you to "be sure to look around your seat and in the overhead compartment for any personal belongings you might have brought on board." If you have just awakened from your nap, it's easy to walk out without something. If you fly from a cold city to a warm city, you can leave your coat behind and never realize it until it's time to go home. One veteran traveler always sets her "trip number." As she leaves home she counts her carryable items. In the winter she has two carry-ons, a brief case, and a coat, so her number is four. At each stop she counts, *one, two, three, four.*

If you leave something on the plane, you should immediately call the airline and give your flight number. If you are on a multi-stop trip, the item may never catch up with you. It is a good idea to ask to have the item returned to your home airport. Of course, if it is your briefcase, you may find it worth waiting. Be sure that all your belongings have your name and address attached. I have luggage tags on my briefcase, my pocket tape recorder, my camera, and anything else that has a handle. I write my name, address, and telephone number with "please call collect" on notebooks, calendars, expense booklets, slide tray boxes, my coat, and so forth. I want to give honest people the chance to return anything I misplace.

Purse Snatchers It's bad enough to lose something, but it's even worse to have it stolen—especially if it's your purse or briefcase. By the way, you should be carrying one or the other: never both. You should always be on guard. Purse snatchers frequent airports and hotel lounges. They know that travelers are carrying more than the average amount to cash.

Never leave your bag unattended. Never hang it on the back of your chair where you can't see it. If you put it under a table, lean it against your leg so you can tell where it is. One of the advantages of a shoulder strap on a briefcase is that you can pull it up over your knee under the table. If you want to take a nap, put your briefcase behind your back. And never, never hang your bag on the coat hook on the back of the door of the stall in the restroom. One of the purse snatcher's favorite stunts is to wait til you are settled and then reach over the door to grab your bag. By the time you get out of the stall, she has disappeared into the crowd. Don't keep all your valuables in one container. If you are carrying a money clip, you will at least have some money left. Keep a list of your charge card numbers separate from your wallet so you can report the loss immediately.

And Never, Never Hang Your Bag on the Coat Hook on the Back of the Door of the Stall in the Restroom.

Bumping Airlines will sell tickets to more people than can be seated on a particular flight. This is to account for the no-shows. Airplane seats are perishable. If that seat flies empty, the revenue is lost forever. But it's not very pleasant to be the person who is left standing at the gate. This is something passengers do to each other. If everyone would call in and cancel their reservations if their plans change, there would be no bumping. Of course, more people would call in if the airlines would set up a special "cancellations only" line so we didn't have to "wait for the next available agent."

The Gate Agents Get to Exercise Some Judgment and Appearance Counts.

One way to avoid being bumped is to arrive in plenty of time. When it comes to passing out seats, the rule is first come, first served. Another precaution is to dress well. You are going to have a much better chance of making your point that it is important that you be at your destination on time if you *look* important. The gate agents get to exercise some judgment and appearance counts. And the airline's customer service representative has even more leeway. If you are at the gate, ask the agent to call back to the ticket desk to summon the customer service representative. Don't walk back there yourself.

If you are bumped, it's critical to know your rights. These are printed in the in flight magazines and available through your travel agent. Here's how United puts it:

> At times, a small number of passengers cannot be accommodated because the confirmed reservations exceed the number of available seats on a given flight. Passengers so involved may be eligible for compensation if all of the following conditions are met: (1) there isn't room on a flight for which you have a confirmed reservation, (2) the flight departs without you, and (3) we are unable to arrange alternate transportation, earlier, or not later than, two hours after, the planned arrival time of the original flight.

The denied boarding compensation ranges from $25 to $200, depending on the price of your ticket. This doesn't help much if you miss a critical appointment. If it isn't important, you might relax and pocket the money. If it is important, be firm. The gate agent can be persuaded to go on the plane and ask for volunteers to deplane for the money. They hold a mini-auction. The right to vacate a seat to accommodate you goes to the highest bidder.

Lost Luggage One of the problems that gets the most press is lost luggage. That is somewhat amazing because a very small proportion of the checked bags are lost. And most of those aren't truly lost. They are temporarily misplaced. They are usually delivered to the owner's hotel room or home within 12 hours of the scheduled arrival time. The airlines really do a great job on this. There are several things you can do to help.

The most important thing is to watch carefully as the agent

fills out the baggage ticket. Make sure it shows the correct destination. Unfortunately, airport codes often bear little resemblance to the city or the name of the airport. There must be some reason why O'Hare is ORD rather than CHI or OHA. Hancock, Michigan, is CMX. These codes are listed in the front pages of the *OAG*. If you aren't sure that the agent is putting down the right letters, make a nonthreatening comment. "My goodness, ORD sure is a funny designation for Dallas. How do you suppose they got those letters?" If the clerk has made a mistake, that comment should bring it to light.

To avoid lost luggage, it is a good idea to check in early, attach a name tag on the outside, tape a business card on the inside, and tip the skycap if you use the curbside check-in. I once stood beside a General Electric salesman at a baggage claim in Boston. He kept muttering, "I knew I should have tipped the skycap." About 15 minutes later we met at the rental car desk. He wasn't carrying any luggage. You should also remove all old baggage tags. An accumulation of baggage tags may make you look well traveled, but it can also send your bag back to your previous stop.

If you're the last person standing in the baggage claim area when they turn off the conveyer belt, your next stop is the baggage office of the airline on which you arrived. They may have your bag stashed in a locker. Baggage handlers go by airline and destination, not flight number. If you checked in really early or if you took a legal connection, one that allows at least the minimum required time period between flights, even though there was an illegal possibility, your bag might have arrived on an earlier plane.

If your bag isn't there, the attendant will ask you for your claim checks and a description of your luggage. They have a sheet with pictures of all of the normal kinds of luggage. You just have to point. They will first check their computer and may well be able to tell you exactly where your bag is and when it will arrive. "Your bag was diverted to Kansas City and will be arriving on American's flight 296 at 3:00 pm. If you'll give us a local address we will have it delivered to you by 5:00 pm." The airlines all cooperate in getting your luggage out on the next flight, regardless of the airline you flew. Unless you have some really pressing engagements, it's a little difficult to ask them for a clothing allowance. You should be traveling in something presentable anyway.

If they can't locate it, they will fill out a lost baggage form. There is an excellent chance that you will get your bags by the end of the day. If you don't, the airline will give you a generous clothing allowance. Your bags are automatically insured for up to $750, but you will have to be prepared to provide an inventory of the contents with a reasonable valuation.

No Room Hotels overbook just like airlines and for the same reasons. They are plagued by no-shows. If they didn't overbook to cover it, the rates would have to go up. If you arrive later in the day, you may find that you have no room. How can you guard against this? It's a good idea to plan to arrive in the early afternoon. Between noon and 3:00 PM is fine. Rooms usually aren't cleaned and ready for the new occupant much before noon. If you think you might be later than 4:00 PM, a confirmed reservation is a good idea. If you change your plans, you can always call and cancel your confirmed reservation before 6:00 PM. This is especially important in high-occupancy cities like New York and San Francisco. Here is a list of the cities where you need to be very careful:

City	Occupancy Rate
New York City	79%
San Francisco Bay Area	77%
Minneapolis/St. Paul	71%
Washington, D.C.	69%
Cleveland	63%
Chicago	61%

(Source: Laventhol & Horwath, "Philadelphia," *Industry Week*, Je 26/78.)

To confirm a reservation, you either have to send in a deposit to cover the first night's bill, give them a charge card number or arrange for direct billing to your firm. Many hotels in resort areas such as Hawaii and Phoenix won't accept your reservation without a deposit. Even if you haven't confirmed your reservation, be sure to write down the reservation number when you make your reservations. If you receive a written confirmation, be sure to carry it with you. You will be in a much stronger position if problems develop.

If you call in and cancel a confirmed reservation, they will give you a cancellation number. Be sure to write this down and hang on to it until the refund appears on your bill. By the way, even if you don't have a confirmed reservation, you should call and cancel if you are not going to show up. It may just make it possible for some other traveler to avoid the problem of finding a room. You'd like it if someone did that for you.

If you are going to be later than 5:30 PM, it is a good idea to call in and ask for the front desk. On the day of your arrival your reservation records are transferred to the front desk and you are no longer dealing with the reservation people. Tell them that you are on your way. You may give them a charge card number at this time to be sure that they hold your room.

If the hotel has overbooked, or if you were late without a confirmed reservation, the Power of Joint Commitment can work wonders. Share your problem with the desk clerk. "What are *we* going to do?" Be sure to be pleasant. The person you are dealing with did not set the policy. Now, in some cases there are rooms in reserve. It depends on the hotel. You must act as if you expect them to find a room for you.

Most hotels have a policy of helping you to find a room. Some hotels will go the limit and pay your transportation to and from the alternate hotel. Be sure that you act pleasantly assertive. Here is the way Western International Hotels puts it:

> Western International Hotels, upon request, will provide you written confirmation of your room reservation. When you have our reservation confirmation and arrive by the time stated, we will have a room for you. If, for any reason, that's not possible, we will secure a room for you in another hotel at our expense, provide your transportation there, and the next day, bring you back to our hotel, where we both wanted you to be in the first place.

If you have any problems, escalate from the desk clerk to the manager. Never accept the answer that there is no manager on duty. There is always a manager on call if not on duty.

When You Are Vulnerable When they talk about traffic safety, they point out that most accidents occur within 25 miles of home. In fact, statistics show that you are more likely to be injured in your bathtub than on the road. But remember, most people spend most of their time within 25 miles of their homes (including time in the tub), than on the road.

You *are* more vulnerable when you travel. The trick is to minimize your vulnerability. You can start by thinking about safe zones and danger zones. Try to fix a little map in your mind. While you should be alert all the time, be especially alert in danger zones. You are usually safe in the hotel lobby, but not in the elevator, parking garage, stairwells, or upper hallways. You are safe inside the airport lobby, but not outside. Be on your guard.

Barbara Jenkins of Braniff Airlines has been to Europe dozens of times. Returning from one European trip, she landed late one night in Los Angeles absolutely bushed. As she left the baggage claim area, a man in a taxi driver cap approached her and reached for her bag, asking if she needed a cab to the city. With her defenses down, she was pleased to have the service. She followed him out the door and across the median strip. When he headed for a parking lot, she started to get worried. Barbara was raised in the South and was carefully trained to be well mannered and polite. She didn't feel right about this, but didn't want to embarrass this man who had been so helpful. With difficulty she said, "Excuse me, but if you're not licensed to operate from the taxi stand, I'm going back inside." She felt badly, but her instincts said, "Watch Out!"

It is important to pay attention to your instincts. If it doesn't feel right, get out. You can avoid many challenges if you keep your eyes open and act on your instincts. If the elevator stops on your floor and you see people inside who make you feel nervous, pretend you forgot something in your room. "Oh shoot, you folks go ahead, I forgot my watch." If you are on the elevator with three people, a couple and another man who makes you feel uncomfortable, and the couple gets off before the man, get off with them. If you are walking down the hall and notice someone standing in a doorway or leaning against the wall, turn around and go back to the lobby. Yes, you may not look friendly, gracious, suave, or all of those other good things, but you will have taken care of yourself and that's much more important.

Choose But Don't Be Chosen.

Another rule is "Choose but don't be chosen." Sometimes you have to depend on other people. When Mary had to reschedule her flight to Long Beach, she found she had no choice but to fly into Los Angeles airport, which is at least 30 miles away. She called the woman who was supposed to pick her up at Long Beach and told her to stay home. Mary intended to get to the hotel on her own. She planned to take the inter-airport bus from Los Angeles airport to the Long Beach airport and then to catch a cab to the hotel. Her plan fell apart on arrival at Long Beach. Not only was the airport closed down for the night, but the local cab drivers were on strike. Now what?

Mary checked out the occupants of the bus. She zeroed in on a respectable looking man in a business suit. "What can I do?" She was pretty certain that no respectable person would leave her stranded in a dark parking lot. And, indeed, he delivered her to the hotel without incident. Of the choices available to her at that point, he was the least threatening. But she had to act fast. If she had waited, she would have been left alone.

Hotels try to provide for the security of their guests, but part of it is up to you. You should heed their warnings and *always* double lock your door when you are in the room. If nothing else, it will save you the embarrassment of stepping out of the shower and coming face to face with the person who has come to check up on a complaint on the color quality of the TV. Many hotels provide peepholes in the guest room doors. Look out the peep hole before opening. Call out, "Who's there?" If you aren't sure, it can wait. Tell the caller to come back later because you just washed your hair. If the caller has a message, it can be slipped under the door. If you open the door for a message, keep the chain on. If it is a legitimate hotel employee, he or she won't mind your precautions at all. And besides, what is more important to you: your well-being or the feelings of a bellhop?

Never put the "Maid, please make up this room early" sign on your doorknob. It says "This room is empty. Burglers invited." If you need to have your room made up, dial housekeeping and request service. If you come back to your room and find anything amiss or feel uncomfortable, don't enter. Go back to the lobby. It's better to leave the bellhops with a story about that "crazy woman who thought there was someone in her room" than a story about the assault on the 22nd floor.

Sickness Travel is fun, but it's also strenuous. It throws off all of your physical and mental schedules. It exposes you to all kinds of people with all kinds of viruses and germs. It means different food, more alcohol, and less rest. You can easily get sick. And being sick is even less fun on the road. Ben Franklin offered the best advice long ago: "Moderation in all things." On top of that, if you are prone to such problems, pack your Bisadol, Kaopectate, and aspirin. Watch your schedule. Be sure that you don't skip too many meals or stay up too late too often. Schedule in a little time to put your feet up.

Moderation in All Things.

If you have any kind of chronic problem such as diabetes, low blood sugar, high blood pressure, or wear contact lenses, you should invest in a piece of "Medic Alert Jewelry" from Medic-Alert Foundation in Turlock, California. It's not quite as pretty as costume jewelry, but it looks respectable. You can buy a pendant that hangs inside your shirt and it won't show unless it's needed. The telephone number is (209) 632-2371. You may not be conscious to speak for yourself and there won't be anyone around who knows you and your condition.

You should also carry proof of both your auto and medical insurance coverage as well as a card with the name of someone to be contacted in an emergency. People have died in the hallways of the hospital emergency room while the staff tried to figure out if the bills would be paid.

If your condition seems serious, call the desk in the hotel or stop at any of the airline counters in the airport. These people are well trained. They are aware of the options and are extremely helpful. You will probably be embarrassed, but that's just the way it goes. When you need help, you need help. You will never see any of these people again anyway.

Car Trouble If you are traveling in your own car or have rented a car, you have some special challenges. If at all possible, it is better to get up early in the morning rather than traveling at night. People who are on the road at 6:00 AM tend to be serious. If you have to travel at night, stick to freeways and well-lighted city streets. Lock your doors. While it's not very sophisticated, a CB radio can be a lifesaver. You can pretend it isn't there unless you really need it. Keep your car in good shape and know some basic car repair procedures. You should know how to change a tire, how to use battery cables, and how to pour gas in the carburetor should you ever run out. Even with the gas crisis, you shouldn't let yourself get into that bind. You should never let your tank get below one-quarter full.

Be very careful with rental cars. You know your own car and its gas gauge. You can't be sure about rental cars. You should never let that gauge get below one-half full. Nancy was driving from Toledo to Akron in a rental car. The gauge read almost a quarter full, but the engine was sputtering. Almost an hour in the sun waiting for road service convinced her that gas gauges can be misleading.

If you have rented a car, check it out before you leave the lot.

It's a pain in the neck, especially when you are in a hurry, but it's really important. Make sure the lights, wipers, and brakes work. Look at the tires. Rental car agencies really try to keep their cars in tip-top condition, but the previous customer may not have been thoughtful enough to report a problem. If you find something wrong with a rental car remember that you are helping another traveler by reporting the problem.

If you have a problem, turn on your hazard lights and stay in the car. Becky was driving home to Akron from her teaching job in Cleveland about 9:00 PM on a warm summer night. Her car started to make a strange thumping sound. She stopped on the side of the freeway just outside the Cleveland city limits and got out to look. Her father had always cautioned her to leave the lights on so she would be seen. She not only left the lights on, she left the car running. Becky was raised in a big city and was a habitual door locker. You guessed it. When she got out she locked her keys inside her idling car.

When She Got Out She Locked Her Keys Inside the Idling Car.

There she stood watching cars whiz by, all alone and feeling very vulnerable. She was watching the on-coming traffic and didn't realize that a car had passed her, pulled off, and backed up to her car. Suddenly she heard someone say, "Are you having trouble?" and turned to see a huge man standing behind her. Fighting panic, she smiled and said in a weak voice, "Yes, there's something wrong with my car." He was extremely helpful. He got out some tools and helped her get into the locked car. He checked it and couldn't find anything to account for the noise. Then he escorted her to a nearby gas station and waited until it was discovered that a section of tread had separated from her tire. She's more careful now. She figures she used up a good share of her lifetime allotment of luck that night. She was absolutely defenseless. They could have found her body in the ditch. She could be dead.

Never leave your car alone in a gas station. When you're in a hurry, it's tempting to pull up to the pump, say "Fill 'er up," and head for the lavatory or the vending machine. That innocent looking attendant can do all sorts of things. He can tug off a wire, twist an adjustment screw, slit a belt or pour some gunk in a fluid reservoir. Now you have both a delay and a repair bill. Wait for the gas to be pumped and then pull your car over to the side of the building and lock it. If the attendant is going to look under the hood, get out of the car and look with him. Never say, "I don't know a sparkplug from a radiator cap." You will be setting yourself up for a rip off. Even if you don't know anything about the car, try to look as if you do.

Unwanted Attention The sight of a woman alone is just too much for some men. There are lots of men who are still trying to boost their egos by scoring with total strangers. A lot of women end up passing up social functions at meetings, foregoing the relaxation of a late afternoon cocktail in the lounge, or eating dinner in their rooms in order to avoid unwanted attention. As Lee Smith of *The Sacramento Bee* says, "They don't seem to realize I'm hungry, not horney."

Even when you're among friends, you can have problems. I was at a professional meeting in the Fairmont Hotel in Dallas. I had been out to dinner with friends and had returned to the hotel for a nightcap. It was crowded, so I ended up perched on a bar stool with my back to the bar conversing with a group of male acquaintances who were standing. Most of the people in the lounge belonged to the association.

A man popped up between two of the people in our group and said, "I need to talk with you." I asked, "Can it wait til morning?" He replied that it was urgent. Assuming that he wanted to inquire about a session or some other professional matter, I hopped off my stool and followed him to a quiet corner. There he proposed certain intimate activities and asked me how much I would charge. I could have been shocked or indignant, but I hadn't done anything wrong. I wasn't going to accept that burden. In my navy skirted suit and oxford cloth shirt, I really didn't think I looked like a hooker! I asked, "How much are you willing to pay?" He answered, "$100." I laughed at him and said, "You're just in the wrong place. I understand you can get the same thing for $50 in St. Louis." I left him standing there looking stupid and went back to my stool. I related the story to my friends and they proceeded to glare him out of the establishment. Of course, this flippant behavior can be dangerous and I probably wouldn't have done it without my friends for backup.

The challenge at a point like this is to make sure that this event which you did not invite does not bother you or cause you to doubt yourself. If you let it get to you, you'll end up a basket case. The offender will go skipping merrily along even though he is the one who is out of place, ignorant, and rude. I didn't know a single thing about the going rates in St. Louis, but my intention was to fling his filthy ball right back into his court.

Besides the sex angle, there seems to be another source of unwanted attention. There are men who are threatened by the idea of equal opportunities for women and will act as if it is your responsibility to account for the behavior of the entire female population. That's a tough assignment.

Nancy found herself being pressed by someone like this at a cocktail party at a convention. It was the old "Well, what do you women want anyway?" routine. She tried all of her normal dodges. "Gee, different people want different things . . . Tell me, how do you like living in Peoria?" and the more direct, "Look this is a party. Can't we talk about something more pleasant?" but he wouldn't let go. She tried snagging another person to join the conversation so she could sneak off. No one wanted to get involved. She finally walked away as he followed with his verbal abuse. She went straight to the host of the party and explained, "I'm really sorry, but I'm going to have to leave now because this guy is bothering me." The host immediately evicted the pest. How do you avoid these unpleasant episodes without cloistering yourself in your room?

You must present yourself as a professional person, both in appearance and in action. You may not be challenged. But if you are, you must not react. If you had an older brother or sister, you already know that a person who doesn't react isn't interesting very long. Practice what I call "selective thick-skinnery." Ask yourself if there is anything for you to gain by answering, reacting, attempting to educate, or even acknowledging the person who has intruded in your space. If the answer is No, put on a thick skin and ignore, ignore! All too often we attempt to be courteous to people who don't even deserve that consideration.

You may want to leave for a minute to make a telephone call or visit the restroom. You may be very direct and say in a calm tone, "I don't care to talk to you." Remember, you can always seek the assistance of a waiter, flight attendant, bartender, or other employee of the establishment. These people want things to be calm and quiet for the other customers.

Amorous Clients It may have started with the traveling salesmen jokes, but all too often it is assumed that a person on the road is interested in fooling around. If it is difficult to deal with total strangers, it's even more difficult to handle advances from people with whom you are supposed to maintain a professional relationship. The two seldom mix.

It may sound paranoid or cynical, but you must be alert to the possibility. Ellen had been calling on a particular buyer for over three years. She had met his wife and children and thought of him as a platonic friend. One evening they were at a business dinner. He was talking about the new house he was planning to build. It seemed very natural when he asked her to stop by his house to see the plans. After all, it was on the way to the hotel. Ellen didn't know that his wife was out of town and that the house wasn't the only thing he had planned.

Ellen Didn't Know That His Wife Was Out of Town and That the House Wasn't the Only Thing He Had Planned.

When they got there he actually pinned her down on the couch and said things like, "Don't you realize that I've wanted you for three years now?" Ellen was absolutely shocked and found herself suffering real turmoil. She had no interest in this man physically, but she had seen him as a friend. She had had no idea of his growing personal interest in her. She wanted to get out of the situation, but she still didn't want to hurt his feelings. Later she marvelled at that. He apparently had no reservations about forcing himself on her despite her protests, yet she was still striving to protect his feelings.

It's a part of the acculturization process. Middle-aged men were raised in an era when NO didn't mean NO. Sometimes it meant "I want to do this but I want you to assume all of the guilt and blame." But Ellen really meant NO. She got out of it by doing two things. First, she didn't struggle. An animal control officer will tell you that in the event you are attacked by a dog, a bear, or other wild animal, you should play dead. You might get a bit gnawed up, but the animal will soon lose interest in you. It's worth a try with humans. It's a pretty good bet that you aren't going to be able to overpower a larger man.

The second thing Ellen did was to repeat firmly and calmly, "No, No, No. We aren't going to do this. This isn't good for either of us. Please take me back to my hotel." He did so sheepishly and she hasn't had anymore trouble with him.

While Ellen was able to maintain her professional relationship with this person, it would have been much better to have avoided the problem in the first place. To avoid these situations, it is critical to monitor your communications. Beware when the conversation turns to personal matters.

Some people claim that flashing a wedding ring helps. I disagree. Some men actually see married women as less risky. A single woman may bring pressures on the man to make changes in his relationships. When the relationship ends, she might cause trouble or call his wife. A married woman would probably be just as interested as he would in keeping the affair quiet. And what if a single woman gets pregnant? Someone is going to get the blame.

Always speak well of your spouse or significant others. Try to keep things on a professional level. Don't let your time with clients turn into pseudo-dates. It often helps to invite his wife to dinner. If he balks at this invitation, it's a red flag. He sees you as a female—not a professional.

Never allow yourself to get into a "you owe me" position. If someone does you a professional favor, send him a present and a note expressing your professional gratitude.

But what do you do if the situation is getting out of hand. First, do not offer reinforcement. If you use the dodge that "this isn't the time or place," it implies that there is some other time and place. You have just set a timebomb. Give a firm, non-ego-threatening rejection. "This isn't good for either of us. It is against my company policy/religion/values/best judgment." Then offer an immediate change of pace: "Let's get back to the party," or "Would you like to stop for a cup of coffee on the way back to the hotel?" or "I'd really like to have some dinner. Would you like to join me?"

You may encounter some situations that haven't been covered here. If you travel enough, something is sure to happen. As you can see, there are a lot of things that you can do to avoid problems. It takes a little creative thought. Try to figure out what might happen, why it could happen, and how you might act to prevent it. If problems do develop, maintain your positive mental attitude, your action attitude, and your self-determination.

Chapter 3
Getting Organized

Nancy knows all about the selection of make-up in the drug store in the Denver airport. She recently had the opportunity to buy a complete set of toiletries during her layover on a trip to New York. None of them were her favorite products, but it was Sunday and she was rightfully concerned that none of the Manhatten department stores would be open that evening. As she paid for the substitutes, she could visualize her carefully packed cosmetic case sitting on the counter at home. The toiletries were replaceable. On an earlier trip she had forgotten her business cards and felt awkward for the entire trip.

Organizing for travel involves setting up a system that will maximize your chances of having the things you need where and when you need them. It means you must anticipate all the requirements of your professional activities. It also means compressing all the dressing and personal care decisions for the duration of your trip into one session. That's what makes it so difficult. You have to make all those decisions at once. It is an exercise in planning, organizing, and decision making. If you can't bring yourself to make decisions, you will end up with everything you own. And the best advice of all travel experts combined comes out loud and clear, LESS IS BEST.

These decisions are tough because they impinge on our inner needs for security. While you really can't bring your teddy bear, you are deciding what little bits of your familiar territory *should* go with you. While you might reason with yourself that you can always buy a replacement if you forget to pack an important item, you can still stay awake in the night reviewing your decisions in your mind.

On a more practical basis, these decisions are tough because of the unknowns. You may not be sure of the weather, the dress standards in the area, available facilities, your clients' specific needs, and other important factors that will affect not only your psychological and physical comfort, but your professional efficiency. You may be tempted to build in too much of an "in case" factor: "Well, I'll take a jacket just *in case* it gets cold, and two extra shirts *in case* I spill something, five more pairs of pantyhose *in case* I get runs, a stapler, some paper clips, a pad of paper, more catalog sheets...."

But those tough decisions will pay off. Remember, each thing you pack will gain both in size and weight during your trip. There are few things that look less professional than climbing back on the plane with objects stuffed in your coat pockets because you couldn't squeeze them back into your suitcase. Being well organized means that you will be able to get your job done better and with less. And you will have more options. One of these is whether or not to check your baggage.

Each Thing You Pack Will Gain Both in Size and Weight During Your Trip.

To Check or Not to Check

Should you check your bags or carry them on the plane? There is no hard and fast answer to this question. If you have a great big suitcase or several bulky sample cases, you have no choice, since there are strict limits on the amount of luggage you can carry on the plane. You may carry on a garment bag, your briefcase, and one other piece of luggage not to exceed 9×13×23 inches. But if you are within the carry-on limits, the answer still depends on several things.

The least important factor is the fear of losing your luggage. According to the Air Transport Association, over 350 million pieces of baggage are checked each year and less than 1 percent of those are lost. Besides, there are lots of things you can do to minimize your chances.

Over 350 Million Pieces of Baggage are Checked Each Year and Less Than 1 Percent of Those Are Lost.

Carry-ons Can Save Time

Time is a more important consideration. Checking baggage takes time on both ends. You have to be at the airport check-in desk at least 15 minutes before the flight. Of course, that's a good idea whether you are checking baggage or not. If you arrive later than that, baggage service is closed. You will have to carry your bag down to the gate. If you are lucky enough to still have a seat waiting for you, an attendant will slip your noncarry-on bag out the side door on the boarding gate and into the baggage compartment. It's really the wait at the arrival end that can make the difference.

The time involved varies. It seems to be inversely related to the volume of traffic. The explanation is simple: During a peak travel period in busy airports, the baggage handling system is at full steam. All of the trucks, conveyors, and employees are on duty. At Los Angeles airport your bags often make it to the baggage claim before you do. But if you come into a low-volume airport or at an off-peak time, the one baggage handler with the one truck may be three planes behind. The baggage hungry passengers can be lined up three deep.

Checking Is More Convenient

It is a lot more convenient to hand over your luggage to the curbside sky cap and pick it up at the curb side baggage claim than to drag it around the airport. This becomes more important if you will be waiting for a while for your flight or if you are in one of the huge airports. But if you use the curb check facilities, be sure to tip the skycap. The normal tipping rates are covered in Chapter 7. Harvey Weiss remembers with dismay the time he stopped at the curb and unloaded two cardboard cartons and two suitcases and handed the skycap $2.00. He says the look on the skycap's face told the whole story. It read, "You really think you're going to get these back at the other end?" It was four days before Harvey's belongings caught up with him.

Another consideration is whether or not you are changing planes. This works both ways. If you are changing planes, you increase your chances of lost luggage. Of course, you also increase the inconvenience of carry-ons. One tip that has been batted around is that you should take the responsibility for transferring your luggage from one plane to the next. The idea is that you should check your bag to the connection point, claim it, and then recheck it to your destination. When you stop to think about that, it's not too logical.

This just doubles your chances of running into problems. Airports are set up for economy of operation—not for passenger convenience. In large airports, the lower level is for arrivals and the upper level is for departures. If you play the double-check game you have to go to the lower level, wait for your bag, go back up to the upper level, wait in the baggage check-in line or go outside to the curbside check station. Then you have to go back through security clearance and get to your gate. That whole process can easily consume 30 minutes. And you still have to get your bag checked in at least 15 minutes before the flight or you will be carrying it to the gate. You need a minimum of a 45-minute layover and everything has to go right on schedule. Do you want to take that chance? What happens if you circle twice and just have time to hurry to your next gate. Your bag will be taking a ride on the carousel while you're taking off. If you trust it to the baggage handlers, it will zip through a tunnel under the concourse and make it to the next gate before you do. And even if it doesn't make the connection, the airline is still responsible for it and will find it and deliver it to your hotel. If you have only checked it part way, it is your responsibility to get it back.

Many serious travelers do prefer not to check their luggage. That's obvious from the crowded condition on the coat closets and overhead storage compartments in the plane cabins. As deregulation and the cost of fuel forces airlines to monitor costs more closely, you can expect that planes will be more crowded. It really doesn't make sense for the airlines to devote cabin space to luggage when the plane has adequate luggage space below the floor. Both squeezing your garment bag into and digging it back out of the crowded closets is often awkward and almost always creates delays in boarding and deboarding. Before you automatically adopt the nonchecking policy, be sure that the 15 minutes is important enough to justify the effort.

Some things shouldn't be checked under any conditions. If you are traveling with sensitive equipment such as tape recorders, projectors, testing instruments, or other electronic gear, keep it with you. The airlines will make you sign a waiver of liability form if you attempt to check these items. Never check irreplaceable items or items that would cause you to be greatly inconvenienced if they were lost. If you are headed to a meeting to deliver a research paper, carry your paper in your briefcase unless you have it memorized.

The Right Equipment

The right packing equipment is very important, since it is both functional and visible. Unless you only do one kind of traveling and always take the same amount and type of clothing, you will need a variety of bags. Selecting luggage is almost as confusing as selecting a car. There are many styles, sizes, and feature combinations. Besides, like so many other things, luggage is becoming very expensive. You probably already have some luggage. After all, it is one of the traditional high school graduation gifts. Look it over carefully to see if it suits your needs as a professional woman.

Appearance In *The Woman's Dress for Success Book* (Warner Books, 1977), wardrobe engineer John T. Molloy gives out a lot of great and tested advice. He says that there is only one type of luggage any woman in America should carry. That is a matched set of tan canvas luggage with brown belting leather strapping. That may well be true, but consider what Molloy is trying to do. He does a very good job of explaining just what clothing and acccessories contribute to a woman's success image. Unfortunately, the reason many of these things are associated with success is because they are impractical. Therefore only successful women can afford to own and use these items. Silk blouses are a great example of this reasoning.

The appearance of your luggage is important. Other people will see you and your luggage and make judgments. If a client or colleague offers to give you a ride to the airport, you don't want to be embarrassed by your luggage. As you check into the hotel, the desk clerk, the bellhop, and other guests will judge you by your luggage as well as your clothes. It can be just the edge you need when you have to speak up about a room assignment, guaranteed rate, early check-in, or error in your billing. It's hard to be assertive if you are standing there clutching a cheap looking bag.

It's Hard To Be Assertive if You Are Standing There Clutching a Cheap Looking Bag.

Tan canvas luggage would leave you with a choice of never checking it or having dirty looking luggage. Baggage handling equipment has this very nasty habit of depositing dark grey tarnish-like streaks on the rough fabric. Beyond that, canvas is considerably heavier than some of the newer nylon luggage materials. Weight is important. You can't count on the availability of skycaps and bellhops.

You may have to make some compromises. You want luggage which, if not high-status designer-autographed, is professional looking. Bags with pink flowers or white vinyl bags with zippered plastic covers scream, "Don't take me seriously." It is a good idea to stick to a plain dark or neutral color. At least it won't clash with your clothing. If you are going to be a serious traveler, you might as well go ahead and invest in good quality luggage in the first place. Aren't you worth it?

Since it must serve a function, there are some things other than pure status or image that are important in your selection of luggage. You must be concerned about factors that affect the suitability of the luggage such as construction, intended use, and features.

Construction The three basic types of luggage are soft-sided, semi-soft, and molded construction. The trend among serious travelers has been toward soft-sided or semi-soft luggage, primarily because it is lighter. When you buy luggage, be very careful about weight. A large molded pullman may weigh close to 15 pounds before you put anything in it. An extra 12 ounces can feel like 12 pounds at the end of a long day. Molded luggage is more appropriate for automobile travel when you will only have to carry it from the car to the motel room.

Soft-sided luggage is lightest and gives the most if you are stuffing it to the absolute limit, but it offers the least protection to the contents. It is the better choice for carry-on luggage. It is not a good idea to check soft-sided luggage. The duffel bag top-loading soft bags are great if you have a lot of squishy or odd shaped items to pack. Just pile it all in and close it up. They are also great if you are the kind of person who totally unpacks at every stop. But if you literally live out of a suitcase for any period of time, you will soon tire of rooting around to find the item that has always squirmed to the bottom of the bag.

Semi-soft luggage has flexible sides stretched over a lightweight framework. It is a compromise on both weight and protection. A rainstorm forced the closing of the Philadelphia airport and temporarily stranded Bernice, who was connecting there on her trip from Hartford to Harrisburg. While she sat calmly sipping her Scotch in the airline lounge, her luggage sat in an open cart on the runway. When she picked it up from the baggage rack in Harrisburg, its navy blue upholstery-like surface was squishy. Fortunately, she had packed a layer of relatively unimportant business papers on the bottom layer and had thrown in several plastic bags of lingerie and laundry just before closing the lid. The papers were pink from the beautiful red quilted suitcase lining, but her tan suit and cream colored shirts were undamaged.

Intended Use Having decided on a construction, you have to select specific pieces. Although the luggage store can look confusing, there are really only four different types of luggage: pullman, tote, cosmetic case, and garment bag. First you should decide which pieces you need and then decide on the sizes and features for each piece.

The pullman is the general purpose piece. Anything you can put in any other piece of luggage can be put in a pullman. If you are only buying one piece, it might be a good idea to get this. The pullman usually comes in small, medium, and large sizes. It is true that clothes for big people take up more room than clothes for little people, but the overriding factor in the size decision is the length of your normal trip. You should only need the largest pullman if your average trip length is more than one week. For shorter trips you should be able to manage with less luggage.

You may not need a pullman at all. Remember, one of the first laws of packing is that the amount packed increases to fill the space available. If you buy a case that is too large, you will tend to take more than you really need. And it is usually easier to manage two medium weight pieces than one very heavy piece.

The Amount Packed Increases to Fill the Space Available.

Cosmetic cases account for about one-third of the unit sales of luggage in this country. But unless you are a model or in the cosmetics business, skip the separate cosmetic case. Most of them are awkward anyway. They are too wide to carry comfortably by your side as you walk. They take up a hand that should be devoted to some more useful piece of luggage or just scratching your nose. They encourage you to take too many cosmetics and personal care products. But worst of all, they clearly label you as a tourist, girlfriend, or other nonprofessional person. LilyB Moskal travels over 100,000 miles a year to her speaking engagements. She says, "I eliminated the cosmetic bag or overnight case because it was too cumbersome to carry and replaced it with a flat, zippered bag which fits inside my suitcase." By the way, the pretty printed cosmetic bags available in cosmetic departments are really more appropriate for the occasional pleasure travel than for the serious professional traveler. With regular use they soon become water stained and wear out. Men's toiletry cases have been designed to last a lifetime. In the long run, a man's case would prove to be the better investment.

Garment bags are convenient. They are very popular with business travelers. They take about two minutes to pack or unpack and can be carried aboard most planes. They are, obviously, best suited to things that can be hung up. While they usually have a couple of zippered pockets, they are not meant to handle two pairs of shoes and a hair dryer.

There are two kinds of garment bags. One has an open top and you supply your own hangers. The second has its own hangers. Unfortunately, some manufacturers call them "dress packs" and assume that all you will be packing is dresses. Their hangers have no provision for skirts. Women's versions are longer than the men's version. If you pack suits, they come about six inches past the center-fold restraining strap, which means that all of the bulk is in the top half of the garment bag. Of course, you could always buy a man's bag, but be sure to get one that folds in half. Otherwise, unless you are six feet tall it will drag on the ground.

Garment bags do not check well. Your crushable garment bag is likely to end up underneath someone's trunk or scrunched in a corner. So you are probably going to have it with you all the while you are in the airport. If you are standing in line you have to hang on to the bag, since they slouch down in a little pile. LilyB recommends a shoulder strap on the garment bag.

Totes are really handy. They are easily carried and hold enough to save you if your checked luggage goes someplace you aren't going. That is only true as long as you don't use it to pack only shoes. Unless it is a really short trip, a tote is a second piece of luggage.

If you are buying pieces one at a time, it is best to start with the medium pullman, add the garment bag, and then get the tote. On overnight trips you can get away with just the garment bag. For two or three days you can take the pullman or the garment bag and the tote. On longer trips you can take the pullman with one of the other pieces.

Features The basic features you should check out in selecting your luggage are latches and locks, wheels, and the type of handles or straps. There are lots of choices.

The idea behind latches and locks is simply to keep your bag closed when you want it closed while making it easy to open when you want it open. If you stand and watch the luggage spin on a baggage carousel, you will soon notice that a well known luggage manufacturer once put out a widely accepted line of luggage with terrible latches. They are always catching on other pieces of luggage and popping open. Test the latches before you buy. Can you open them easily yet have some confidence that they will stay closed in transit? Watch out for recessed latches. They are murder on long fingernails. It took one woman who bought a recessed lock bag about seven fingernails to learn to search for a key or pen to pop her latches. And be careful of zippers: They can ruin pantyhose or sheer fabrics.

Airline agents strongly recommend that you always lock your luggage. Theft isn't the only reason. Locks give you added protection against your latches springing open and indiscreetly spewing the contents of your suitcase across the entire baggage carousel in front of a hundred people. Locks are also useful if there are a few things that you will be leaving in your hotel room. A locked suitcase is a better place than on the table. Of course, for the real valuables it is wise to make a trip to the front desk and make use of the safety deposit boxes there. Too often people don't lock up because they don't want to bother to search for the key. And many poor travelers have had the misfortune of losing their luggage keys. Combination locks are the best bet. They can be set to any number you choose. Pick a favorite date—perhaps your birthday—and you'll never be locked out.

The wheel was one of the world's greatest discoveries. That goes for luggage wheels too. Little metal strap-on wheel carts are fine for boxes and small bags, but do not work well with large bags. Buy those with their own wheels attached. You can get wheels attached if your favorite type doesn't come with this feature. It is much easier to drag your luggage than to carry it. Of course, this only works on hard smooth surfaces. Luggage with four wheels is much more stable than luggage which must be tipped to roll on two wheels.

The problem with wheels is that you can become dependent on them. You may be tempted to pack so many things that you end up with a suitcase that you can't handle on stairs. It's embarrassing when you ask someone to help you lift your suitcase off the carousel and get, "What do you have in this thing? Rocks?" Bellhops and cabbies will glare at you as they strain to lift your bag.

In the Hartford airport there is only one escalator and it is normally set to carry passengers upstairs. Bernice was on the second floor and had to go down to the first floor. She couldn't handle her bag on the stairs. She had to go to the desk and ask to have the escalator reversed. Then she had to endure the impatient looks of a few upward-bound would-be escalator-riders.

When PSA only flew within the state of California, you could not check a bag through to United, American, or any of the other national carriers. When changing from PSA to United in San Francisco, Sandra claimed her bag and found that one of the four wheels had been knocked off. She had to drag her lopsided bag scraping along the concourse for almost half a mile. When you really need one, a skycap can be hard to find. Of course, one problem with wheels is that you have to put up with all the comedians and their, "Hey Lady, what do you feed that thing?" jokes.

The normal choices on handles are single handles, double over the arm handles, and shoulder straps. The obvious benefit of shoulder straps is that you can manage to get your hands free. But some people keep their hands so free that they look like they are going to strangle themselves. Shoulder straps can absolutely ruin the line of your jacket.

Some People Keep Their Hands so Free That They Look Like They Are Going to Strangle Themselves.

Maxine liked her shoulder strap tote so well that she bought a larger carry-on bag with a strap. She found that the weight on the strap gave her a headache. Shoulder straps are fine on small totes, but when it gets to the two-suiter sized bag, they are a hazard. Don't buy a larger bag with a shoulder strap unless it has a regular handle as well.

Careful Planning Pays Off

Careful planning is the key to being an organized traveler. This planning begins long before your trip. One way to plan is to get in the habit of preparing two lists: a trip list and a packing list. A list forces you to be more organized. The pencil is an amazingly powerful tool.

Your Trip List A trip list is simply a day-by-day accounting of your appointments, obligations, and arrangements. Write the days and dates in the left hand margin and begin to list all of the details that will be important to you in accomplishing your objectives. These include the people you are to see along with their telephone numbers and addresses, your hotel arrangements, your flight numbers and times, restaurant reservations, and anything else that you might forget. For example, if you are to meet someone for lunch on Tuesday, Monday would include an entry to call and confirm those arrangements. It is so easy to forget important details in the hustle of traveling. Remembering those details will substantially improve your travel efficiency. Keep your list handy and add to it as your trip plans are developed. Another useful practice is to use the back of each trip list to make a "to do" list for that trip. You may need to make reservations, contact people, accumulate papers, replenish supplies, and so on. You will also find that this list will be useful as you fill out your expense report or in the event that you are audited by the IRS. You will know where and why. Obviously, you will want to carry this list in a convenient but safe place.

Your Packing List Organizing continues with the construction of a packing list. Start by analyzing your expected activities during your trip. If you are going to a seven day company meeting and expect to see the same people day in and day out, you will need more variety than you would need if you were going to be gone the same seven days but stop in seven different cities. As Ann Boylan of American Airlines says, "As long as you feel personally clean, who knows that you've been wearing the same suit for three days?" Will you be going to both social and business functions? Are you planning any recreational activities? Will it be cold? Will it rain?

If this is your first trip to a city or to a particular type of event, you might want to seek some advice. Cheri Marshall joined the National Speaker's Association and was about to attend her first national meeting. All of the conference brochures stressed the casual dress and outside activities. That seemed to fit, since the meeting was in recreationally-oriented Phoenix in the summer. But as a professional woman attending a professional meeting, she was still uncomfortable.

So she got in touch with Pat Fripp, a woman who had been to the meeting the previous year. Pat confided that although many of the people were in very casual clothes, she had been more comfortable in her suits. Cheri packed dresses and suits and was pleased that she did. While there were hundreds of people at the meeting and the majority were in casual clothes, all of the officers and well known people in the organization were wearing business clothes. Some of the men were even wearing vests!

LilyB says:

> Packing need not be a chore if you have planned your wardrobe ahead of time. That means wise and careful buying until you have accumulated the desired traveling wardrobe. I like tailored suits, but you have to find out what makes *you* comfortable. I dare not be overdressed. It is better to look tailored than provocative.

You should plan your packing several days before your trip. That will give you time to wash, take clothes to the cleaners, get a new pair of black pumps, or do all of the other odds and ends. Of course, it's better to take LilyB's lead and keep your wardrobe ready at all times. To accomplish this, have everything cleaned and ready to go again as soon as you return from your trip.

Sit down far from your closet with a piece of paper. Draw three lines dividing the paper into four columns. In the first column make a list of expected activities. If you are going to a convention, you might want to consult the program to see what events are planned. Leave a couple of lines between each activity because you will need the vertical space when you get to the second and third columns.

Then in the second column, start to fill in the major pieces of clothing which seem most appropriate to the activities on your list. Do this from memory. That way you will end up taking the things you like the best and in which you feel the most comfortable. If you start pulling things out of your closet and draping them all over your bed, you will end up taking far more than you need.

Think about weather. You can check the national weather

reports in the morning paper to see what it might be like at your destination. If you are traveling from Los Angeles to Green Bay, Wisconsin, in February, it's hard to remember how cold it can get. Each time you write down a different piece of clothing, look down the rest of your list of activities to see if there is some other place where that particular piece could be used again. Stick to a basic color scheme. Things will go together in more combinations and you will need fewer pairs of shoes.

Most professional women find that they end up taveling with much the same wardrobes as professional men. The basic pieces of clothing for a five day trip would include:

Two skirted suits (preferably navy, grey, or black)
A contrasting skirt (tweed, herringbone, small check, etc.)
Five Shirts
A basic dark jersey dress in the same color range

This prepares you for formal business with the full suits, more casual business with the contrasting skirt, and dinner in the dress. Of course this is just the framework for your packing. The suits look entirely different when set off by different accessories. I have my suits made with detachable buttons. I can switch the buttons on my black suit from black to silver or gold and turn it into an evening suit.

In the third column list all of the accessories you need to go with the pieces of clothing. Remember lingerie, scarves, shoes, belts, jewelry, purses, and stockings. Remember, try to find additional uses for each item. You don't need seven sets of lingerie or seven shirts just because you'll be gone a week. Women are fortunate in that their lingerie can be easily hand laundered and dries quickly. Besides, any cleaning or laundry that you have done while you're traveling on business is tax deductible. Be especially careful about shoes. Try to limit yourself to two pairs.

Finally, in the fourth column, make a list of all the miscellaneous items. You can start from the outside and work inward moving from coats, gloves, umbrellas, to deodorant. Some women start with the morning and work through the day to brushing their teeth before climbing into bed. The trick is to be systematic and consider all of the things you do in a normal day. Be sure to tuck in some comfortable clothing to wear when you are alone in your room in the evening—something between business suits and nightgowns. Joan Kennedy, a professional speaker, always takes her favorite robe. "It takes up space, but it's comfortable and warm and it makes me feel at home." Don't forget an emergency kit including a spot remover packet, soap flakes, aspirin, a tiny sewing kit, a safety pin, scotch tape for lint removal and quick hem repairs, and a travel alarm. Ruth Cleary offers a good tip: after losing several travel alarms, she has finally drilled a hole through the plastic case of her new alarm and chained it to the handle of her briefcase.

A couple of envelopes of instant soups will be worth their weight on that night you arrive after room service has been closed. Ann Boylan packs a ziplock bag of instant coffee. "I hate to wait for room service in the morning." A couple of tea bags will not only give you a pick-me-up, but if you lay down with damp tea bags over your eyes for a few minutes in the afternoon, you'll be in better shape for the evening.

Now, turn the paper over and make your nongrooming list. This includes everything that isn't a part of your personal care and grooming. Start with your wallet and money, your airline ticket, business cards, hotel reservation confirmations, conference program, business papers, personal telephone book, and work your way through including everything you need to accomplish your mission.

Be sure to have proof of your insurance coverage. If you should be in an accident in another city, you may need proof of coverage to get adequate treatment. If you take medication or wear glasses or contacts, tape a copy of your prescription inside your suitcase and carry a copy in your wallet. Set your list aside for a while. Then go back and review your choices. If it still looks good, you are ready to begin the physical part of packing.

Packing Techniques

The objective in packing is to have your belongings arrive at your destination in the best possible shape. But you may make a few compromises based on your type of travel. If you are going to a single destination where you will stay for a period of time and then return home, you will only pack twice. Therefore you can use one of the full suitcase packing systems. But if you are on a tour of one night stands, it can get to be a real pain to have to totally unpack and repack at each stop. You will want to adopt some practices that allow you access to items without a total unpack/repack cycle, yet still keep your things in reasonable condition.

One Stop Packing The most commonly recommended method of one stop packing is nested folding. You use the suitcase for a packing guide. The best way to encourage creases is to fold each item of clothing separately. There is nothing to cushion out the creases. Twenty years ago women used to stuff their clothing with tissue paper for this reason, but that seems highly impractical today. Instead, use clothes to cushion other clothes. Lay your largest item in the bottom of the suitcase hanging out over the side. Then lay additional items on top, each at right angles to the last. The idea is to avoid having all of the waistbands or collars stacked on top of each other, or in other words, to distribute the bulges evenly throughout the bag. After all of the larger pieces have been laid in the bag and are hanging over all four sides, smaller items are deposited in the center. Then the hanging edges of the clothes are folded over the top.

Whenever possible, try to fold along natural body lines. For example, it's better to fold a skirt at the hip line than the hemline. If you use this packing method correctly, each item of clothing ends up curled around other items rather than being folded flat and creased.

Don't attempt to defy gravity. Heavy things like shoes, travel irons, and hairdryers should be placed opposite the handle where they are going to end up anyway. Try to balance these side to side and front to back to make it easier to carry your bag. Shoes should be put in some type of mitt. You can buy special shoe mitts or use old athletic socks, but try to avoid plastic bags since they might mark the leather.

Plastic bags are a good idea, however, for cosmetics and other liquids. Even if the liquid is in a plastic bottle, it is a good idea to enclose that bottle in a plastic zip lock bag. Dale wears contact lenses. She has to have distilled water for the sterilizer unit. She carries the distilled water in a plastic baby bottle. She once picked up her suitcase at the San Diego airport only to find that it was leaking. While the distilled water didn't cause much trouble with her clothes, it was a little embarrassing.

Just imagine how it would have been if Dale's shampoo had leaked instead. Even with pressurization, the lower air pressure at high altitudes allows liquids to expand. It is a good idea to fill plastic bottles only two-thirds full and squeeze out some of the air to allow for this expansion. Pump sprays travel better than aerosols.

Cosmetics are a big factor in the weight of your luggage. Don't take full size bottles of anything. Look for small sizes of your favorite products. But don't buy unfamiliar products just for size. Transfer your favorites to small plastic bottles and jars. It can make pounds of difference.

Multi-Stop Packing If your travel takes you to several stops on one trip, you will need some shortcuts. One is to pack your lingerie in bundles according to use. Pack all of the items you use to get dressed at one time together. Instead of having a bag of pantyhose, a bag of bras, a bag of slips, and a bag of panties, you have a bag for each day of your trip and each bag has one pair of pantyhose, one bra, etc. It saves time dressing and it saves time repacking since you leave all but one of the bags in the suitcase.

If you will be living out of your suitcase, you may want to become a roller. The rollers learned their system from the Navy. On board ship it is important to fit the most in the least space. There is no doubt that a roller can fit more into a suitcase. The process is simple. You smooth the various items out on the bed and roll them up like logs. Then you stack the logs in the suitcase. Rollers claim they avoid creases and can pick out individual items from amongst the stack of logs.

Another trick is to pack in layers. Of course, suitcases are not constructed in layers so you have to construct your own. All you need is a large piece of fabric. If you want to get fancy, you can fold and stitch it then stiffen it with a piece of cardboard. You pack all of the accessories and nonclothing items in the bottom of the bag as evenly as possible. Then you lay your fabric on top. Using a variation on the folding method, lay your skirts in first, all in one direction, your jackets next, and vests or folded shirts on top. Fold the jackets and skirts back over the vests and then fold in each of the four sides of the fabric to form a bundle. Now you can lift this bundle out and get to things in the bottom of the suitcase. You never need to unpack the lower level. Regardless of how you pack, the two last things to throw in are your packing list and your business card. If your luggage tags are lost, they will still be able to identify you. You can use your packing list to be sure that you come home with everything.

Saving Time Proper packing is time consuming, but there are some ways to save time. One tip is to save your lists from one trip to the next. Be sure to note the date and the place. If you can really discipline yourself, you should make notes on your old lists. *Never used extra sweater.* The next time you will think twice before packing it. Even if you don't make notes, it will spur some recall of what did and didn't work out. And your list of cosmetics and nongrooming items may remain unchanged from one trip to the next. Eventually you will have it perfected.

Another tip is to leave your bag partially packed. If you are a frequent traveler, it pays to have a travel hair dryer, a set of travel cosmetics, a travel umbrella, and duplicates on other frequently packed items that live in your suitcase between trips. You should also store shoe mitts, zip lock bags, and other packing aids right in the suitcase between trips.

Getting organized takes some time. It requires evaluation and decision making. But the time spent in organizing for your trips will pay off in terms of increased efficiency. It's better to take the time to plan when you are at your desk or at home than to be caught trying to patch up mistakes in unfamiliar territory.

Chapter 4
From Point A to Point B

In science fiction movies the heroine steps into a telephone booth-like contraption and is molecularly transferred through time and space. While that seems like a great idea, we still have to settle for cars, planes, busses, cabs, and other less exotic means. There is, however, a lot that can be done to make the best use of the available options.

Air Travel

Flying is the fastest way to travel from point to point. The problem is getting to the starting point and away from the ending point. With increasingly crowded airports, parking problems, preflight waiting times, baggage claiming delays, and driving time to and from airports, flying may not save you any time unless you are headed for a place over 200 miles away. Then you still have to arrange for ground transportation at your destination. But for longer trips, flying is the only reasonable answer. It costs more than surface transportation, but you have to consider the value of your time.

Reservations There are two ways to make reservations. You can either call the airlines yourself or you can call a travel agent. Bob Schulman at Frontier Airlines says that the best tip he can offer the serious traveler is to deal with professionals who specialize in travel arrangements. It doesn't cost any more to go through a travel agent. The airlines pay them a commission on their sales. Otherwise airlines would have to have thousands of extra employees to handle ticketing. LilyB Moskal says, "Select a good reliable travel agent. They are worth their weight in *gold!* Several times when I was due to catch an early morning flight and had failed to pick up my tickets, my agent has called to remind me." Travel agents offer convenience. If you give them your credit card number and a signed authorization, you can even handle all of your ticketing by phone and have the tickets mailed to you.

It Doesn't Cost Any More to Go Through a Travel Agent.

Some people choose to deal with the airlines directly, based on the belief that the airlines hold out a few extra seats. They think that a travel agent's computer might show that a flight is full, whereas the airline could give you the last seat on the plane. That may have been the case before the widespread use of computerized reservation systems. There was no way to keep all of the travel agents up-to-the minute on seat availability. But things have changed. According to Ann Boylan, Advertising Director at American Airlines, the travel agent's computer gives the same information as the airline's computer. There are no hold-outs. That makes a lot of sense. The airlines want the seats sold; they don't care who sells them.

There is one advantage of dealing with the airline directly. Most major carriers have special computer-tracked programs for frequent travelers. People who spend more than a certain dollar amount—say $750—per quarter are included on a mailing list of "Frequent Travelers" and receive newsletters, inflight discount coupon books, and other special benefits. The airlines keep track of your account according to your telephone number. Unless the travel agent gives your telephone number to the airline's computer, you won't get counted. Some agents withhold this information either because of the bother or because they are afraid that the airline will grab their business. You should make it clear to your agent that you want your telephone number listed. There is a second reason to insist on this: if airline personnel are aware of an impending problem, they will attempt to contact you. For example, the plane scheduled for your flight may be delayed in another city because of equipment or weather problems. If they have your phone number, they will try to advise you to take a different flight or at least warn you to delay your departure for the airport.

Just like any other service business, travel agencies vary in terms of specialties and service. Some agencies specialize in vacation tours and cruises. Others cater to the business traveler. While a smaller agency might offer more personal service, many of the larger agencies have on-line computer tie-ins with the airlines and are able to check availability and confirm reservations during the time you would have been sitting there listening to recorded music while you waited for the "next available airline ticket agent." As deregulation complicates travel arrangements, we can expect the demise of the friendly neighborhood travel service. Computer facilities and other sophisticated services will become critical.

Within an agency, you will still be dealing with an individual. It is to your advantage to establish a business relationship with one agent who will then be more aware of your travel patterns. For example, some travelers have more flexibility. The agent then knows if it's worthwhile to suggest alternate routes or extending the stay by a day or so if it would result in lower fares. It pays to try out a few agents until you find one you like. The question is, what can you expect from your travel agent?

Above all, you should expect accuracy. There is nothing like showing up at the wrong time or the wrong day because somebody mistyped a few numbers on your itinerary. Beyond that, the more you travel the more you can expect. Airlines can increase fares on short notice. If you have reservations but have not yet purchased your tickets and a fare increase is announced, you should expect your agent to notify you so that you can buy the tickets and avoid the increase.

How soon should you make reservations? It is to your advantage to make your reservations as soon as possible. With deregulations and increased fuel costs, the airlines have cut down on the number of flights and many flights are sold out. If you hope to take advantage of any of the many discounts plans, you have to get in early. The number of seats available at these lower fares is limited. When they are gone, there are no more. If you actually pay for your tickets, you guarantee yourself the fare even if the rates are increased before your trip. If you must change your itinerary after you have purchased your ticket, you are still eligible for the low prefare-increase rates as long as you do not change the first flight on your itinerary.

Fare Negotiations Airplane fares used to be confusing, but with deregulation and increased competition balanced against increased fuel costs and shortage of airport space, the fare situation is becoming impossible. One reporter called seven different times on the same trip and got five different fare quotes. Even conscientious travel agents have trouble keeping up with all of the special fares and discount requirements.

Here are some of the tips you can use to get the lowest possible fare. If you consider the economic situation facing the airlines, they make a lot of sense. The airline is trying to fill up more seats and reduce its risk. That's important to you as a traveler, since it is one of the ways airlines can keep costs and prices down. Therefore, the earlier you are able to make your reservation, the better off you will be. By promising the airline that one of its seats will be filled, you have reduced its risk.

Shop around. When fares were regulated, a trip between point A and point B cost the same regardless of the airline. Today different airlines charge different prices so it pays to compare. Except for flights during prime time where airlines have established cooperative fare arrangements, it can save you money if you stick to one airline. Not only do you offer them more revenue, but costs such as ticketing and baggage handling are reduced.

The airline has lower risks on high traffic routes. Flying from San Francisco to New York will cost less than a flight from Sacramento to New York, even though Sacramento is closer to New York. Check to see if you can begin or end your flight in a larger city, but don't forget to figure in the value of your time and the cost of surface transportation.

There are so many discounts and the requirements change so frequently that you will have to check with your travel agent for the latest details. The place to start is by asking your travel agent to look for a "Q fare." The Q is the discount designation. Then you can check to see if you can meet the restrictions. Here are some of the points that are often included in the restrictions. You may have to buy your ticket 30 days before the flight. You will probably not be able to change your departure date once you have purchased your ticket without paying additional fare, although you may have some flexibility on a return date. You may have to stay over at least seven days. Or you may just have to stay over at least one Saturday night.

You may be limited to two stopovers. If you have to make

more than two stops, ask your travel agent if the discount allows for an open jaw. That means that you arrive at one city and depart from another city. It is assumed that you are going to take ground transportation between those two cities. You may do that, or you may buy a second ticket independent of the first ticket and make a couple of stops in between. If you do have to go to several cities, check to see if any airlines are offering passes. These are tickets sold at a fixed price that entitle you to unlimited flights on one airline over a specified time period. Of course, you can only go to the cities serviced by that airline.

First Class vs. Coach Most flights offer both first class and coach. While both sections of the plane arrive at the same time, there are differences to be considered in making your choice. Many companies will only reimburse for coach travel. Some people choose to pay the upgrade out of their own pocket.

First class is more expensive, but there are some advantages beyond free drinks, cloth napkins, and larger seats. It starts with special first class check-in counters. There is seldom a line. Once on the plane, the first class beverage service begins before take-off. One big plus is that you have a better chance of avoiding screaming kids. Parents are people, too, and surely most of them try to keep their children from bothering other passengers, but a coast-to-coast flight next to a cranky kid can be a real trial. Even a short trip can be a pain. Margaret, an advertising account executive, was flying from Los Angeles in a tan suit to visit a client in San Francisco. A young woman in jeans and T-shirt with a toddler sat in the next seat. The toddler was clutching a soggy graham cracker. The mother seemed oblivious to the fact that the child kept flailing out at her seatmate's skirt with the soggy cracker. It's hard to be polite when a child hangs over the seat in front of you, kicks the back of your seat, or races up and down the aisle for 2000 miles.

You Have a Better Chance of Getting an Interesting Seatmate in the First Class Cabin.

You have a better chance of getting an interesting seatmate in the first class cabin. It may even be a celebrity. Some airlines run a business class section. For a small surcharge on the normal coach fare, you get to sit in a special "quiet zone" away from the kids, jeans, and paper shopping bags. A woman who is in the management consulting business flies first or business class on the chance she might run into some new business prospect. But if you are a serious nonsmoker, the problem with the first class is that the cabin is too small to be divided effectively.

Connections There are four kinds of flights: nonstops, direct flights (stopovers without a plane change), intra-airline connections (plane changes to the same airline), and inter-airline connections (plane changes to a different airline). If it is at all possible, try to fly nonstop. A nonstop may leave later and arrive earlier. Be sure to check both departure and arrival times before you select a flight. It can be worth your time to drive 100 miles to a major airport to avoid time consuming connections.

The necessary connection times vary greatly. On a direct flight, you can relax and enjoy it. Unless it's a real long layover or your need is desperate, you should stay on the plane. If you deplane and don't make it back, you can be in trouble. For this type of flight you only get one ticket coupon. You will be left with only a boarding pass for a departed flight.

When you have to change planes, you have more to worry about. There is a list of legal connection times printed in the *OAG*, the telephone book-like directory of airline schedules used by travel agents and others in the travel business. These are estimates of the minimum allowable time between flights. The idea is to get both you *and* your baggage on the next plane. For example, 45 minutes is the minimum allowable time for a connection between a United Airlines flight and a Braniff flight at Newark airport. In airports such as Atlanta, O'Hare, John F. Kennedy, Los Angeles International, and Dallas/Ft. Worth, it can take 30 minutes just to walk to your next gate. If you add 15 minutes for boarding and a few minutes to pass through the security screening, an hour layover evaporates.

Most travel agents recommend allowing about 30 minutes more than the minimum legal connection time. Of course, if you have carry-on luggage and are an Olympic-class sprinter, you can book reservations with legal connections and still try to make it to the gate in time for that flight under the minimum time.

It's stress-inducing to be circling an airport and checking your watch, knowing that your next flight is scheduled to depart shortly. If the airport is backed up because of traffic delays or weather, there is a good chance that your next flight is delayed as well. If you are late arriving because of a late take-off, you might be thinking about an alternate plan. Do check with the flight attendant though. If there are quite a few passengers who are trying to make the same connection, airlines have been known to hold the plane a few minutes. It's worth a try.

It's really depressing to miss your connection and get stranded at an intermediate airport. During the United strike in 1979, I was traveling from Norfolk, Virginia, to Sacramento, California. United is the principal carrier for both of these cities. To make things worse, I had to fly on a Saturday, a day when fewest flights are available anyway. That meant I had to catch a plane in Norfolk at 6:00 AM EST, transfer in Washington D.C., fly to St. Louis, catch another plane to San Francisco, and then wait another two hours to catch the final flight home arriving about 6:00 PM PST. The total trip consumed 15 hours or about three times what it would have been without the strike. It only takes 17 hours to fly to New Zealand. I had an hour layover in St. Louis, but my plane arrived exactly an hour late. I ran all the way to the next gate only to find that the other plane was also delayed. Even though I felt a little foolish, I didn't feel one-tenth as foolish as I would have had I arrived to watch the plane pull away without me.

You may be left on the ground through no fault of your own. Sometimes the airplane has a mechanical problem. People get angry about this, but think about it. Wouldn't you prefer to stay on the ground if the plane isn't working properly? Margaret waited for a half an hour while mechanics replaced the pilot's seat. She never did find out what was wrong with it, but if he wasn't ready to fly, neither was she. Western Airlines treated all of the passengers to a free drink in appreciation of their patience.

I was flying from Dallas to Sacramento via Denver in February. Dallas and Sacramento were both having beautiful weather, but Denver had a winter storm. We were an hour late getting into Denver because of the traffic back-up. But my next flight had also been delayed, so I thought I'd make it with only a slight delay. I did call home, however, to caution my husband to check with the airline before starting for the airport. Barbara Jenkins of Braniff Airlines recommends that you never leave for an airport without calling ahead—regardless of whether you are the passenger or the reception committee.

The phone call was a good move. The next plane boarded at the rescheduled time, but it was going to be a long night. De-icing planes is important because the extra weight of the ice can cause a crash. Halfway through process, the de-icing tank truck ran out of fluid. It was almost an hour before it got back with a refill. In the meantime, simply running the electrical system on the airplane depleted the fuel supply, so we had to wait for a refueling truck. Than it was a wait for clearance on the runway. The passengers got to sit in their seats on the ground for over two hours. and guess what? Frontier treated everybody to a free drink. Voila!

Weather is a big problem in many areas of the country. It may be clear blue skies and sunshine where you are, but if the plane you are supposed to board is coming in from another city that is having weather problems, you may be delayed. Julie was in Chicago in January. It was cold, but it was clear. She didn't bother to check the airport before leaving her hotel. But when she got to O'Hare, she thought someone had turned the clock back to Christmas Eve. People were sleeping on the floor among the crowds. It seems that bad weather in New York had grounded all of the planes that normally stop in Chicago on the way to the West Coast. All she could do was wait with the rest. Some airports always have delays simply because of the volume of traffic. This is especially true in hub airports: O'Hare, Atlanta, and Denver.

The point is that you can never be sure that your original flight plan is going to work out. Therefore, if at all possible, don't cut things too close. Allow yourself a back-up. It's better to arrive in town a few hours early than to be calling to say that you aren't going to make your appointments. Always allow yourself a back-up and know what it is in advance.

Serious travelers carry their own pocket-sized copy of the OAG, the *Official Airlines Guide*. This is the book that lists the facts on over 27,000 flights over the most frequently traveled routes in the U.S. and Canada. As Richard Nelson of the North American Guides puts it,

> You need your own source of schedule information rather than being at the mercy of the airline you are flying. While airlines generally do have all the schedule information, some may not be willing to provide this information until they have had an opportunity to sell you on their own services.

And it can simply be a matter of time. If the airport is crowded and there are 20 other people in line ahead of you, you can be standing there waiting to get information while the plane you need is boarding elsewhere in the airport. The subscription to Pocket OAG costs less than $3.00 per month. You can get the latest information by dialing 800-323-3537.

Multi-Airport Cities Some cities are serviced by more than one airport. The major airport receives long distance flights and smaller regional airports receive flights on shorter hops. If you are flying from Houston to Dallas, you can fly from downtown Hobby Airport to downtown Love Field and avoid about 60 miles of traveling on the ground. If you fly into New York City, you may have a choice between LaGuardia, Newark, and Kennedy airports. In the Los Angeles area you can go into Los Angeles International, Burbank, Orange County, or Long Beach. In San Francisco you get to choose among San Francisco International, San Jose, and Oakland. In Chicago you can avoid O'Hare and hop a flight out of close-in Midway airport if your destination is one of the nearby Midwestern cities. Since flying to the regional airport could save you both dollars and time, be sure to ask your travel agent about it.

Red Eyes Some people hate to waste a day traveling and swear by "red eyes," those planes that leave the West Coast sometime after 10:00 PM and arrive in East Coast cities around 7:00 AM the next day. They reason that they save the cost of a hotel room, can travel during otherwise wasted time, and even save money on the flight. Just stop for a minute though and look at two facts. They are called "red eyes" because you end up with *red eyes*. Beyond that, the lower price reflects the collective opinion that the middle of the night is not the most pleasant time to fly. Therefore, the airlines offer price incentives to fill up some of the seats. In fact, some people brag that they fly first class for coach rates and "freedrink" themselves across the continent. First class can be important if you are a large person, but if you drink too much on one of these flights, you're just going to waste a day on a hangover aggravated by jet lag.

> **They Are Called "Red Eyes" Because You End Up With Red Eyes.**

Red eyes are a gamble. Sometimes the plane is almost empty and you can stretch out across three or four seats and sleep. At other times every seat is filled and you get to try to sleep sitting up. No one can sleep well sitting up. Even if the plane is empty, you may encounter rough weather in which case the flight attendant will be waking you up to put on your seatbelt. Check to see if your red eye will be making stops. For safety reasons, the flight attendant will wake you up for both landings and takeoffs. Even when you are in smooth air, you have no control over the environment. Just one crying baby is enough to turn a nightflight into a nightmare. And even if you don't encounter any problems, you are going to have to choose between boarding the plane with a clean face or sleeping in your make-up, a practice skin experts abhor.

When you arrive in the morning, you will usually have trouble checking into a hotel. Most hotel rooms aren't cleaned and available until after 11:00 AM. Some airports, such as the Phoenix airport, have pay shower and dressing rooms adjoining the women's restroom. Slip two quarters into the Nik-o-lock slot and you have a chance to refresh. But changing or fixing your make-up in a public bathroom is less than luxurious.

Sometimes you have no choice. If you are traveling coast to coast, you soon learn that planes do not leave the west bound for the east between 2:00 and 9:00 PM. To do so would mean arriving between 11:00 and 6:00 in the morning—highly undesirable. If you can't get free by noon, you'll never make the earlier flights and will have to add another day to your trip.

I learned this the hard way. I was scheduled for a luncheon meeting in San Francisco one day and an early afternoon meeting in Allentown, Pennsylvania, on the next day. The only way to do it was to take the red eye. I did my best to handle the situation. First, I arranged for a late check-out at my San Francisco hotel. After the luncheon, I went back to my room and took a nap. Then I showered, dressed in an easy fitting velour dress with minimal undergarments, and went out for a light dinner on the way to the airport. I arrived at the gate a half-hour before the flight and got a seat assignment in the center section of the widebody plane, hoping to have the row to myself. When it turned out that way, I got out my cosmetic bag and made a quick trip to the lavatory where I washed my face and brushed my teeth. Back at my seat with the cabin lights out, I coiled my long hair onto a few rollers and settled down to sleep with the pillow and blanket I had collected early in the flight. Remember this: The pillows go fast so get yours early. The blanket is equally important. At about 3:00 AM you start to feel chilled.

I was doing well to this point, but my best move was that I had set up a confirmed hotel reservation in Allentown for the night of the flight. Yes, that's right. I was paying for a room I wasn't occupying. But when I arrived at 8:00 AM, I was sure I was going to have a room available. I checked in and went to bed until noon. I was going to do my best to be fresh for my important meeting.

Special Meals Comedians do jokes on the quality of airline food. It's true that you will find better food in a quality restaurant, but for the most part, the airlines do an exceptional job of feeding people in the sky. Consider the problems involved in feeding 200 people both hot and cold foods and beverages with no real kitchen. Think of the number of meals these food services put out each day. Some of those people who try to impress you by downgrading the airline's meal probably don't eat as well at home.

One of the things the airlines do very well is to provide special meals, but you have to request the meal when you make your reservation and, of course, take the flight you reserved. Some of the special meal categories are vegetarian, low sodium, kosher, Indian, high protein, low calorie, soul food, Hindu, and diabetic. If you have a dietary concern, be sure to speak up when you make your reservation. It is also helpful to the flight attendants if you identify yourself as having ordered a special meal when they are serving the premeal cocktails.

Safety Meals, movies, magazines, and all of the other trappings of air travel are only a front. The most important factor is safety. Airlines are concerned with your safety above all else. Even the critics of business and the profit-orientation of the American Business System would have to admit that the airlines are very interested in getting that airliner and its highly trained flight crew between point A and point B safely. If nothing else, the plane itself costs from $10 to $20 million dollars.

What can you do about safety? First, be cooperative with airline personnel who are imposing safety precautions. Being indignant when they ask to hand search your luggage or making jokes about hijacking or crashes isn't becoming. When the flight attendant asks you to push your bag a little further under the seat or asks to take a large or awkward piece to the back of the plane during the flight, be understanding. Too many passengers ignorantly say, "Oh, it won't bother me." The flight attendant doesn't care about your legroom. The idea is to keep the aisles clear so that the plane can be evacuated quickly in an emergency. If you have your tray table down or your seat back reclined during take-off or landing, you are blocking someone's escape route. They aren't fooling when they instruct you not to put heavy objects in the overhead racks. In case of turbulence those heavy objects could come crashing down on someone's head.

No matter how many times you have flown, you should pay attention to the brief safety demonstration. If nothing else, know the location of the two exits nearest your seat. Every once in a while, take the time to read the instructions on how to operate the emergency door and slide. Don Korn, Editor of *Business Travelers' Report,* urges the readers of this newsletter to learn the best positions to assume in an emergency landing. There are survivable crashes. Don't be aggravated if the flight attendant wakes you for take-off or landing. That is so that you will be ready to take action if necessary. For this reason, the airlines will not board an obviously intoxicated person. The American commercial airline industry has a great safety record. These carriers have well developed safety programs, but passenger cooperation is still the most critical element.

One traveler did something that could have ended up in the papers. Ed had arrived early for a flight from Chicago to Dallas. While he was sitting in the boarding area he was approached by two well dressed women who asked, "Are you taking this flight to Dallas?" He replied in a friendly manner, so one of them went on to explain that she just had to get a package delivered to her company in Dallas. "If you could carry it with you, I could call my boss and he'll meet you at the gate in Dallas." Now Ed is a nice person. He wants to be pleasant and helpful and basically believes that people are honest and good. He agreed to carry the package. The woman thanked him and went to the phone to call her boss to describe Ed.

Ed boarded the plane, it took off, he was having a drink, and then it hit him—THUD. His thoughts raced, "What is really in this package? It could be a time bomb. It could be an extortion plot against the airline. They might be calling in the ransom demand right now." He could almost hear it ticking. He panicked. He started to perspire as he dug in his pocket for his nail clippers. The package was neatly wrapped and taped with that nylon reinforced tape. As he was agonizingly clipping at the tape with his little nail clipper, the flight attendant noticed him and asked what the problem was. Fortunately, he finished just as she did. Had he not already unwrapped the package, there is a good chance that the attendant would have confiscated it and notified the captain. In that case, it's probable that the plane would have been ordered back to O'Hare causing not only delays, but the mobilization of emergency services, possible accidents, and Ed's arrest. It was a stupid thing to do and he was very lucky. It was a videotape cassette just as the woman had promised. At this point his only problem was explaining the appearance of the package to the woman's boss.

Con Artists and Other Criminals Can Pick a Patsy and Prey on Well Intentioned People.

The moral is simple: Don't agree to do extraordinary favors for strangers. Con artists and other criminals can pick a patsy and prey on well intentioned people. Unfortunately, bad people can put up a good front. Ed should have refused and advised these women of the airline's small package express service. It would have cost them about $15.00 to put the package on the plane legitimately. Had Ed given them the $15.00 himself it would have been money well spent.

During the Flight   Between take-off and landing, flying can be boring. There are some things you can do to make yourself more comfortable. It starts with seat selection. United, Pan Am, and some other airlines publish the seating plans for their planes. Many experienced travelers have favorite seats and ask for them by number. Taller people tend to prefer the emergency exit rows where there is more leg room. These rows also tend to be a few degrees cooler because of slight drafts. Be careful of the row in front of the exit row since the seats may not recline fully. The same is true of the last row in the cabin. If you have carry on luggage, you will want to avoid the front row since there is no place to put it. If you are a serious nonsmoker, try to stay at least four rows away from the smoking section. If it is a movie flight, find out the name of the movie before selecting your seat. It is quieter in the front of a plane and the ride is smoothest in the center over the forward part the wing.

If you plan to sleep, you will be better off in a window seat or in one of the center section seats of a widebody. No one will be climbing over you to get to the aisle. Otherwise most experienced travelers opt for the aisle seat. It offers you more freedom to move around the cabin. It is a rare person who can do serious work on a plane. Ann Boylan says she never travels without a really good book to pass the time. Cavett Robert, one of the most respected public speakers in the country, uses his hours of plane time to write letters with datelines like, "May 31, 1979, between Chicago and Phoenix." He always carries his address book and stationery. If you forget your paper, there is a supply on the plane. Planes also carry playing cards if you have a partner or are a solitaire freak.

Flight attendants do their best to make you comfortable. When there were fewer professional women traveling, there was some basis for the charge that women travelers were treated with less consideration or respect. That is not at all true today. It is true, however, that not all passengers are treated alike. To a great extent, this is due to the passengers' behavior.

Here are some things that drive flight attendants up the wall. Some people never smile or say thank you. Others don't have enough sense to stay out of the aisles during beverage or meal service periods and end up climbing around the carts. There is plenty of warning about the beverage or meal selections. They announce it on the PA and have it printed on a menu, a napkin, or on a seat pocket card. People still ask, "What do you have?" It just delays the service for everyone else.

If You Want Good Treatment on an Airplane, All It Takes Is a Little Common Sense and Consideration.

A real aggravator is the person who rings the call button for a coffee refill or a magazine during the service periods. The attendants are required to stop and answer that call just in case the person is sick or in real trouble. Again, it slows down the service for everybody else. Time is usually very limited, and flight attendants are periodically graded on their serving efficiency. If you want good treatment on an airplane, all it takes is a little common sense and consideration. Flight attendants can be very helpful and friendly.

Special Considerations There are some days when you have a higher probability of running into problems. Among these high problem-potential days are Sunday afternoons when everybody is headed out and Friday evenings when everybody is trying to get home; at least two days before and after every three day holiday; a week before and after major holidays; and bad weather seasons.

San Francisco and other parts of the northern West Coast can be fogged in for days in December, January, and Feburary. Chicago and the rest of the Midwest are targets for blizzards in the winter. Keep these problems in mind as you plan your trips.

Another interesting detail that will escape notice until it hits you is the "K flight." These flight designations are in the airline guides. K flights are cancellable flights. If there aren't enough people on board at departure time, the airline can cancel the flight and let you wait for the next scheduled flight without being penalized. There you sit. These flights are scheduled for low-traffic periods or low-traffic cities. Be careful.

Airline Lounges For about $30.00, you can get a membership in one of the airline clubs. Most airlines have them. Men have been joining them for years. They are at least as useful for women travelers. You can join at the club desk in the airport or ask your travel agent or airline representative for information. Here is a list of the clubs:

Airline	Club	Annual Dues	Life Membership
American	Admiral's Club	$45	$450
Braniff	Council Rooms	$30	$300
Continental	President's Club	$35	$300
Eastern	Ionesphere Club	$40	$400
National	Sun King Club	$40	$350
Pan American	Clipper Club	$40	$400
TWA	Ambassador's Club	$35	$500
United	Red Carpet Club	$35	$350
Western	Horizons Club	$40	na

These clubs offer a lot of services that can be important to you in your travels. They offer a relatively safe and quiet refuge in the airport. They have comfortable places to sit and relax with a cup of coffee or a drink. You aren't going to be hassled by the petition peddlers or the beggars who cannot be prevented from soliciting in airports. While they don't serve meals, they often serve rolls in the morning and crackers with cheese in the afternoons. If you are a diet soda drinker, airline clubs are one of the few places where diet soda is available in the nation's airports. There are TVs and magazines, nice lavatories, quiet telephone booths, conference rooms, and other business travelers who can be good company. There are very few children and they can't stay if they are pests.

The airline personnel in the room can help you with your tickets, seat assignments, and boarding passes so that you bypass the desk at the boarding gate and go directly on the plane. You can also receive messages at the club. This can be important if people are trying to get through to you while you are in route. Club members are respected as frequent travelers and are issued special reservations phone numbers so that they have a better chance of getting through to make reservations.

The clubs also offer an opportunity to advertise your professionalism. You get luggage tags which other serious travelers recognize as a sign of a frequent traveler. To be able to say to a half-way interesting seatmate, "Gee, if you have an hour layover, I'll buy you a drink in the Red Carpet Club," puts you in a commanding position.

In fact, your membership may end up being free. Through membership in airline clubs you are exposed to all kinds of special offers. These clubs negotiate discounts with rental car agencies, special two-for-one offers with hotels and fine restaurants, and other arrangements that can save you money. If you are serious about joining a club, be sure to inquire about life membership rates. Once you start to travel, it's hard to stop. Rates of clubs, just like everything else, are increasing.

Jet Lag Many people feel tired and irritable after coast-to-coast flights. It can upset your circadian rhythm. Our bodies get accustomed to certain schedules. When you skip across three time zones, it takes a while to adjust. The problem is even worse with an international flight. Jet lag is a real disease. The symptoms include loss of appetite, constipation, headaches, sleepless nights, confusion, and exhaustion. If you fly to Europe, it can really hit you hard. In fact, most business travelers will not conduct any business on their first day after a transatlantic flight.

People have different levels of tolerance to changes in time zones. If your life is irregular anyway, it will cause you fewer problems. But if you run according to the clock, you may want to take some precautions. Try to get plenty of rest before you leave and to arrive at your destination close to your normal bedtime. Get some exercise during your flight. It helps the circulation. Try to eat, drink, and smoke very little, if at all. The effects of alcohol are greater with the high altitude and low humidity of jet travel.

But drink plenty of water and fruit juice.

For the first couple of days, you may try to eat your meals according to your hometown clock. But be careful about your watch. Ed Thomas learned the hard way. He left his watch on Chicago time when he went to New York. In the hassle of the day, he checked his watch and forgot the time difference. He arrived at LaGuardia at 4:30 PM CST to catch a plane that had departed at 5:00 PM EST. His advice: "Always change your watch to the local time."

Ground Transportation

The three factors to consider when choosing ground transportation are cost, time and convenience. Your first challenge is getting from the airport to the hotel, but you must also consider your responsibilities while you are in town. If you are attending a convention in a downtown area, you may want to stick with cabs throughout your visit. If you will have to travel around within the city, renting a car may be the answer.

With Someone Else at the Wheel The basic ground transportation choices are cabs, hotel busses, bus services, and airport limosines. But check the options. In Washington you can take the shiny Metroliner to and from the airport for a ridiculously small charge. In Long Beach you can catch the city bus in from of the airport and ride downtown for 25 cents. Some cities offer excellent public transportation networks: Kansas City, Atlanta, and San Francisco are examples. In many cities you will find the bus route map in the telephone book. It takes a little more effort than a cab, but if you aren't on a tight schedule, it might be worth it.

Cabs are usually the most expensive option. But the question is, "How much more?" Do not hesitate to ask the dispatcher or driver for an estimate. Remember to consider your time and convenience. Spending less may end up costing you more. And here's another point to remember: Not all cabs have the same rates. For example, O'Hare is considered to be part of the City of Chicago, although it is located in the western suburbs. Chicago cabs that service the area charge the metered rate to take you to Chicago or to a limited number of "approved suburbs." If you take a Chicago cab to an unapproved suburb, you will have to pay one-and-one-half times the metered rate. However, there is a suburban cab stand at the airport. If you take a suburban cab, you pay only the metered rate. It pays to ask before you hop into a cab.

Spending Less May End Up Costing You More.

One woman arrived at Los Angeles International airport and had an appointment about an hour-and-a-half later in Westwood Village near the UCLA campus. The trip to Westwood takes about 20 minutes. In this case a cab would cost $11.00. The airport bus service would drop her off within a block of her destination and only cost $3.50. The hitch was that the next bus wouldn't leave for 45 minutes. Her question was whether she should sit on the bench at the airport and save the $7.50 or take the cab. She waited for the bus. She arrived at her destination just five minutes before her appointment having walked a block dragging her luggage. She didn't have time to check into the hotel so she had to drag her suitcase to the meeting. In retrospect she realized that she would have been a lot better off to spend the extra $7.50 if for no other reason than that she would have had time to freshen up and review her notes before the meeting. Her time was certainly more valuable than that.

If you are taking an airport bus, be careful of the bus route and drop-off order. If your hotel is the driver's first stop, you only have to worry about the preloading time since the travel time will be about the same as in a cab. But if the driver is making other stops before arriving at your hotel, you can build in about three to five minutes per stop. That can add up to a significant delay.

Busses can have some other advantages though. One of them is a certain sense of security. Ruth was on her way to a home economics symposium when she climbed into a cab in Atlanta, Georgia, and asked the driver to take her to the Hospitality Inn on Desert Drive. He responded, "The only Hospitality Inn I know about isn't on Desert Drive. It's on the Crosstown Freeway," As he started off from the airport, she checked out her hotel confirmation slip and sure enough it read 1501 Desert Drive. For about $8.50 in meter tickings she sat there wondering what she was supposed to do about the fare if he was taking her to the wrong place. It turned out that the driveway-like turn-off from the freeway to the hotel was indeed named Desert Drive. When you take a bus it goes to a specific destination that is usually noted on the placard on the side and leaves little doubt.

What do you do if a cab driver does take you to the wrong place? In many cities such as New York and Miami, a high proportion of the cab drivers speak English as a second language. That can be a problem. Kathy Kordas reports that she got in a cab at the East Side Bus Terminal in New York City and asked to be taken to the Sheraton Russell Hotel at 55 Park Avenue. The driver was having trouble with the language and she didn't know the city well. He took her to the corner of Park Avenue and Fifty-fifth Street. When she realized she was in the wrong place, she stayed in the cab and repeated the directions. The meter read about $4.00 instead of the $2.00 it should have been. What should she have done? She gave him $3.00 and he was happy. It had been an honest mistake.

In another case, Lynn had taken a friend to dinner at Commander's Palace, a very nice restaurant in New Orleans. They were taking a cab back to the Hilton Hotel and were talking pleasantly when Lynn noticed that they were on Bourbon street in the Vieux Carre, the French Quarter. They hadn't asked for the scenic route, and the Vieux Carre is not on a direct line between the restaurant and the hotel. At this time in the evening the driver had fewer chances of picking up fares and was taking these two presumed-to-be-ignorant tourists on a little tour to run up the meter. In her most assertive voice Lynn demanded that he turn off the meter and proceed directly to the hotel. There she paid him the same amount that had been on the meter on their earlier trip from the hotel to the restaurant. Later she regretted the fact that she had not taken his medallion number and reported him to the company. This does point out one precaution. While most drivers are friendly, helpful, and honest, it is usually a good idea to refrain from comments such as, "I've never been to New York City before..." or "I really don't have any idea of how to get to the hotel..." Remember, there are still lots of people out there who assume that women are ignorant and we don't have to reinforce those attitudes.

When you take cabs to and from the airport or within the central district of a city, you can be reasonably sure that you aren't going to get stranded. But if you take a cab to any place out of the normal flow of cab traffic, you should ask the driver about getting back. Sometimes the driver will offer to wait for you. If you ask the driver to wait, you should pay for waiting time. It's about 10 cents per minute. If the driver offers to wait, the meter should be turned off.

If you don't know your way around and have a lot of appointments at various places in the city, you may be better off to rent a limousine. You can get a chauffered Cadillac limousine to take you anyplace you want in metropolitan Chicago for about $20.00 per hour. You have to sign up for a minimum of two hours. But if you had three appointments at scattered points and then returned to the hotel, the same trip could easily cost you $80.00. Besides, you would have the anxiety and delay of waiting for cabs. The limousine is certainly impressive. And if you have luggage, you can leave it in the limousine rather than dragging it into someone's office.

Many hotels run hotel busses. Holiday Inns and Ramada Inns are really good about this. When you make your reservations, be sure to ask about service to the airport. These busses are handled in two ways. If the hotel is quite a distance from the airport, the bus usually runs on a schedule—for example, every hour on the half-hour. Those closer to the airport tend to run on demand. When you have picked up your bags you call them, usually from a display of hotel advertising with direct line telephones located near the baggage claim. It is important to have picked up your bags before you call since delays at the baggage claim can cause you to miss the bus. The advantage of these busses are that they are convenient, they are free, and they don't get lost. There can be wrinkles. A lot of these busses don't exactly stop and wait to see if anyone wants to go to their hotel. It seems like they slow down slightly and you get to hop on.

Bernice called the hotel from Bradley Field in Hartford, Connecticut, only to be told that the bellhop hadn't shown up for work and there was no one to drive the van over to pick her up. "No, we don't know when he will be in." The hotel was about 15 miles away, but she decided to take a cab. Then she found out about the shortage of cabs in Hartford. In cities like Chicago and Los Angeles, the cabs are lined up waiting. But in Hartford you put your name on a list and wait. They expected to be able to get her a cab in about 30 minutes. Clearly, that was unacceptable. Since hitchhiking seemed out of the question, Bernice called the hotel and pleasantly but firmly explained that she was going to find someplace else to stay unless someone managed to pick her up. She also managed to mention that she found this problem to be surprising, since the major insurance firm for which she was doing some consulting work had strongly recommended their hotel. Seeing both current and future revenues flying out the window, the desk clerk managed to cover for the bellhop. This strategy could have backfired if the demand for hotel rooms in Hartford was so strong that the hotel was able to fill that room and other suitable hotels were booked.

Rides to and from airports can be a problem. I once arrived home a day early. Knowing the delay at the baggage claim, I stopped on the way down the concourse to call home so that someone could pick me up. No one was home. I found myself standing beside my seatmate as we waited for our bags. It had been a three hour flight and in my fatigue I sighed, "Darn, no one is home so I guess I'll get to wait here." Gallantly, he offered to give me a ride. I accepted.

As We Crossed the Bridge Over the River, He Turned Right On the Exit That Led to the Deserted Park on the River.

It was about 9:00 PM. My normal route home went through the center of town, across the river, and down another freeway. As we crossed the bridge over the river, he turned right on the exit that led to the deserted park on the river. "Oh-oh, I'm in trouble now..." flashed through my head. I scanned my options: jumping out of the car, waiting to see what happened, screaming, warning him that I'd put up a fight.... With self-control I said quietly, "What route do you take to the east side?" He calmly explained that he took Richards Boulevard to Del Paso Boulevard to I-880 to Arden Way, and so forth, and proudly pointed out that it cut five minutes off the driving time. While I arrived home safely, I have had second thoughts about accepting rides from strangers.

Renting a Car If you have a fine sense of direction, can read maps well, and have to make a lot of stops in town, a rental car may be your best bet. There are some cities where it is almost a necessity. Dallas, Houston, Los Angeles, Detroit, and Phoenix are cities that are so spread out you could spend a fortune on cabs. Downtown San Francisco and the Loop in Chicago, on the other hand, are so compact that most people walk. A car is a real handicap in Manhattan.

The basic advantage of renting a car is the flexibility it offers. You can come and go as you please. If you have a car, you are in control. If you are in someone else's car, you can become a captive. Betty was attending a conference that was held at the Nevele Country Club near Ellenville, New York. The Nevele is a self-contained resort with all of the meals, facilities for everything from ping-pong to horseback riding, and a nightly stage show.

During the early evening Betty was talking with some salesmen who were also at the conference. They were interested in going to a different hotel a few miles down the road where "they have a better band." They wanted her to go along. She knew them slightly and was willing to go, but was very clear on the fact that she had a very important meeting the next morning and had to be back at the hotel by midnight. Off they went.

They needed two cars since there were eight people. The first stop was about five miles away. Guess what? The band had the night off. Well, the Disco Danny of the group knew of an even better place just a little bit further down the road. Betty reiterated her intention of being back at the hotel by midnight. That brought up a few "turn into a pumpkin" jokes, and the group was off. Much to Betty's distress, this ride lasted about 25 minutes. That meant she was at least a half-hour from the hotel in rural upstate New York and it was already 10:15.

There Was Betty in her Navy Blue Suit with Seven Guys in a Topless Joint. Great!

The place turned out to be a real dive. They arrived during intermission. Things went from bad to worse. It was a topless dancing operation. There was Betty in her navy blue suit with seven guys in a topless joint. Great! She tried to keep her composure and sat there for almost an hour. Then she turned to the man next to her and asked, "Which one of you guys is going to take me back to the hotel?" His answer was, "It's not my car." She turned to the guy on the other side and the answer was, "I never promised to get you back."

When word spread around the table, Disco Danny swaggered over to her and whispered that he'd be willing to take her back. Of course there was a catch. Since he was staying with one of the guys who would be staying behind, he wouldn't have any place to stay. "I'd have to stay with you." That was too much. Betty excused herself and headed for the telephone. There is no Yellow Cab Company in Fallsburgh, New York. She went to the manager and asked which of the local cab drivers might care to get out of bed to drive her back to the Nevele. The manager was aghast. "That would cost you at least $40!" By this time one of the men had been struck by a severe case of guilt. He came over to say that he had the keys to one of the cars and would take her back. Betty turned down his offer. She waited for the cab and paid the $40.00 plus a generous tip. The next morning when she went into the meeting, she felt self-confident and self-reliant. There were seven men who couldn't look her in the eye. If it had been Betty's car she could have bailed out at any point in the evening. If they didn't want to come along, they could have walked back.

The costs of renting a car vary greatly. The rate structures are almost as confusing as airfares. Rental car rates are also very negotiable. Rental car hours are just like the airplane seats. If no one buys them the revenue is lost forever. Therefore there are all kinds of discounts. You can get discounts because you belong to various organizations, because you are a business traveler, because you belong to an airline club, or for lots of other reasons. Your auto insurance company may have negotiated a rental car discount arrangement. Check it out with your agent. There are even discount coupons in the in-flight magazines and on your ticket envelop. Bill Ellis at Weinstock's Department Stores says, "Never pay the published rate."

There are three components to the bill: the basic daily rate, the mileage charge, and the insurance coverage. The daily rate depends on the type of car you rent, the day of the week, and the number of days you keep the car. Smaller cars usually cost less, but most car rentals won't give you a confirmed reservation on a sub-compact. The demand for cars is greatest from Sunday night to Thursday afternoon. Therefore the car rentals offer weekend rates. They are interested in the full utilization of their fleets, so are willing to give you a price break if you promise to keep the car for a week or longer.

Car rentals usually figure a certain number of "free miles" into the basic daily rate. Most people don't drive that far and the rental is better off to charge you a higher flat fee than a lower flat fee plus mileage. On weekday rentals these miles are limited to around 150. Weekend rates and weekly rates may have unlimited mileage. If you drive much more than the limited free miles, have the clerk figure your bill two ways—first, with the days plus the excess mileage, and then with enough extra days to cover your mileage. If you went 150 miles over your mileage limit on a car with a mileage charge of 20 cents per mile and a daily rate of $20.00, that would save you $10.00 (150 miles × .20 = $30).

While you are checking on possible discounts, be sure to ask your travel agent if your own auto insurance covers you in a rental car. If you sign up for the rental car company's per day collision and personal injury insurance, it can add close to 25 percent to your bill.

You will pay a premium if you return the car to a place other than the place where you rented it. Car rentals are franchise operations. Each outlet owns its own cars. If you turn it in at a different place, someone has to pay to have it returned to its owner. The extra charge will be something like 20 cents for each mile from the renting location plus a fee of $15.00. So plan ahead. I had several appointments in New York City on Wednesday and Thursday. I arrived at LaGuardia on Tuesday afternoon and took a cab to the city. On Friday morning I was to call on IBM in White Plains, which is about 25 miles north of Manhattan.

On Friday morning I took a cab back to LaGuardia rather than picking up the car in midtown Manhattan. Then I drove out to White Plains. Later I continued on to Boston to spend the weekend sightseeing. On Monday I drove back to Hartford, Connecticut, for an appointment and then back to a northern suburb of New York City for the night. Mid-Tuesday morning I drove through New York City to LaGuardia where I turned in the car and caught my flight to Atlanta. The rental car bill from Friday morning to Tuesday morning was only $100.30. Flying from New York to Hartford would have cost about $90.00 and I would have been stuck with no transportation. A little planning saved me a lot of money and having the car over the weekend saved me from the severe depression that could have struck if I had had nothing to do over the weekend.

Rental car rates and discount programs are changing constantly. The only way to keep up on these changes is through a frequently published newsletter such as the Business Traveler's Review. You can subscribe to BTR at $48 per year. The address is 210 E 52nd Street, New York, NY 10022.

Obviously, careful planning can help you to move your body from point A to point B with the minimum of hassle. It may not be molecular transformation, but it beats a covered wagon. Getting there can be half the fun.

Chapter 5
Your Home
Away From Home

Your hotel room becomes your home away from home—your haven. It's the place that gives you security. If you feel uncomfortable in the night, you can't do a good day's work. Comedian David Brenner was explaining the problems he has when he is traveling: He gets homesick. Some people try to do something to make their hotel rooms more home-like. They bring a picture or buy a flower. Brenner claims it is easier to take the opposite approach. He says he's made his apartment in New York more like a hotel room. He screwed the radio to the night stand, folded the end of the toilet paper into a triangle, and put a chain lock on his bedroom door.

> Different Sounds, a Different Bed, and Worst of All, an Unfamiliar Pillow, Can Combine to Bring an Attack of Insomnia.

Many travelers complain that they have problems falling asleep on their first night on the road. Part of this is due to the excitement of travel itself, but unfamiliar surroundings don't help. Different sounds, a different bed, and worst of all, an unfamiliar pillow, can combine to bring on an attack of insomnia. While you'd feel a bit odd carrying your own pillow into a hotel, there's a lot you can do to be sure that you are in the hotel that best meets your needs.

Selecting the Right Hotel

Your hotel room is your base, your home away from home. In most cases it's also your office away from home. It serves as your contact point, your storage area, your work space, and your refuge. Therefore, at least four factors should be considered in selecting a hotel: convenience, safety, status, and cost. Your priorities will depend on the purpose of your travel and may easily change from one night to the next. If people will be calling you, picking you up at the hotel, or expecting to be able to discuss business at your hotel, the status factor takes priority. As with most other things, status and cost are closely related. The trick is to select a hotel with the status that meets your needs.

A high class hotel may charge more than twice the normal room rate of a standard hotel in the same city. If it is important that you present a high class image, that alone may justify the increased cost. If you are in town to make a high level presentation to a major corporation, you may not want to give out the phone number of a budget chain as a contact point.

But the difference isn't all in image. A big part of the difference is accounted for by service. A full service hotel has to devote more space and more employees to nonsleeping room activities. All of this increases costs. In a standard chain motel you will find no room service, limited restaurant facilities, and a rack of maps of local attractions. If you want a cab, you can call one from the pay phone in the lobby. Services at a high class hotel usually include:

- A doorman to take your bags to the registration desk
- A bellhop to escort you to your room
- Full room service on a 24-hour basis
- Dry cleaning and laundry services
- A variety of restaurants and lounges
- A concierge to answer your questions
- Evening maid service (with a candy on your pillow)
- In-room movies
- Complimentary overnight shoe shining
- The morning paper
- Health club facilities or privileges
- Goodies like shampoo, bubble bath, shower caps
- Conference and meeting rooms with AV services
- News stands and gift shops

Some of these features are simply pleasant, but several of them can make your stay much more secure. In most full service hotels the bell station is adjacent to the guest room elevators. There are also a number of employees on duty on the floors or at the main desk throughout the night. This does a lot to discourage loiterers. Having a selection of pleasant restaurants within the facility allows for a pleasant dinner without leaving the hotel. Many of the newer full service hotels are being constructed in conjunction with shopping malls, theaters, and convention facilities. You can go out in the evening without going out.

Another trade-off is between cost and convenience. Your need for convenience is affected by choices on other travel matters. For example, if you have decided to rent a car, it may be just as convenient to stay in a less expensive motel outside the city instead of a centrally located expensive hotel. You can meet your clients at their offices or at a neutral point, so your address is less important.

Hotels are convenient because they are close to your appointments, are close to transportation, or have all of the services you need. If your time schedule is tight, it will be important to have a hotel room close to the places you need to visit. If you were going to call on brokerage houses near Wall Street in Manhattan, you wouldn't want to stay at any of the hotels in Midtown. It's not only the cab fares but the time that's important. But you also have to consider nonbusiness activities. The Midtown hotels are closer to shopping and the theater district. Would you rather take long cab rides during the daytime or late at night?

Long Distance Phone Calls Are a Real Bargain When You Compare Them to Missed Appointments or Acute Aggravation.

When you consider location, be sure to check your schedule of activities. A publicist once had the foresight to set it up for an author on a book promotion tour to stay in the Howard Johnson's right next to the television station by the Charles River in Boston. That's just super, except for the fact that the author's first interview in the morning and last interview in the afternoon were miles away in downtown Boston. She was back near her hotel room at 1:00 PM and didn't even have enough time to stop in and brush her teeth. That author knows better now. She checks her schedule against the map and makes her own reservations. If she isn't sure of a location, she calls and asks. Long distance phone calls are a real bargain when you compare them to missed appointments or acute aggravation.

Airport hotels thrive because of the transportation angle. They are just the thing for a really short stay. Say you are arriving one evening, going downtown to appointments the next morning, and flying out that afternoon. By using an airport hotel, you can get into your room a lot sooner. The next morning you can check your bag with the bell captain and avoid dragging it around to your appointments. You may even check your bag with the airline. At O'Hare, DFW, and many other major airports, the hotel is across the street from the ticket lobby. Even when the hotel is a short distance away, it can be better to get up a bit early so you can grab a cab to the airport and check your bag and then take a cab or limo downtown. That way you can go straight from your last appointment to the airport. Be careful though because some airlines do adhere to a preflight baggage check-in maximum time limit. You can get around that if you check your bag with the skycap at the curb. If he questions it, just tell him that you are going in to change over to an earlier flight. Your bag will get out on the next flight and be waiting for you when you get to your destination. It will give you peace of mind if you limit this stunt to trips when you are headed for a secured baggage claim area where they require matching claim checks. Unless you have scheduled meetings in the hotel, you wouldn't want to stay too long in an airport hotel. Airports are always out in the middle of nowhere, and you get to listen to planes all night long.

If you are attending a convention, it is always worth the price to stay in the main conference hotel. While you may save a few dollars by staying at a satellite hotel, you miss out on a lot of the unofficial activities that mean so much. If you attend evening cocktail parties or social functions, you open yourself up to dangers traveling back to your hotel. If you just want to sneak off during the day; if only to go to the bathroom in private, you are out of luck.

At one meeting at the Hyatt Regency in Memphis, late registrants, or those trying to save a few bucks, were housed in a hotel only a few hundred yards away as the crow flies. Unfortunately, it was on the other side of a major freeway interchange. The cab ride, when you could get a cab, was about $2.00. You don't have to do that many times to make up the difference in room rates. Be sure to get your reservations in early since the main hotel fills up first.

If you are going to a conference, be sure to mention that when you make your reservation, since your group may have arranged for a special rate. Hotel costs are increasing just like everything else. The rate you pay is tied to the demand for hotel rooms in that city and for that hotel in particular, the services offered in the hotel, the quality of their rooms, the convenience, the status of the hotel, and the type of room you reserve. You may actually reserve a lesser room and be given a nicer room depending on the availability of rooms. If you have a confirmed reservation at a particular rate, you should not pay a higher rate regardless of the room to which you are assigned. If a suite is all that they have left, that's the hotel's problem.

Some people deliberately play the odds. They make a guaranteed reservation and plan to show up after 6:00 PM, the time when most hotels will no longer honor unguaranteed reservations. By this time the desk clerk will have assigned most of the standard rooms and may only have suites left. Since the hotel knows it is going to get your money for that guaranteed reservation whether or not you show up, the standard rooms may be rented to people who walk in off the street with no reservation. These people don't have any money up front and are more likely to go elsewhere if the clerk offers high-priced suites only. This scheme can backfire if the hotel really runs out of rooms. Then you will be heading for another hotel.

Holiday Inns, Inc. did a survey and concluded that 70 percent of the people registered in hotel rooms on any given night have never stayed in that hotel before. Most people are buying a pig in a poke when it comes to hotels. Our author friend above arrived in Dallas late one night and headed for the hotel room which had been reserved sight unseen by the same Chicago publicist. She was a slow learner, but she knew she was in trouble when there were no doormen or bellhops. If she had known how much trouble she was in, she might have stayed in the cab.

She Was in a Dump Full of Transients and Other Undesirables.

When she was checking in, a man across the lobby called out to the desk clerk: "Hey, you be sure to wake me up by 5:30

tomorrow morning. I want to get down to the hiring hall early just in case there is some work." She was in a dump full of transients and other undesirables. At 1:30 AM in a hotel with no doorman or cab line, her options seemed limited. She had an 8:00 AM appointment less than a block away, so she closed her eyes and put up with it.

How can you reduce your risk? Information is the key. One source of information is your contact at your destination. If you are calling on a customer or visiting your company's plant in a distant city, ask the person you are calling on to recommend a place to stay. This works better if your contact does a lot of business with people from out of town. After all, people seldom patronize the hotels in their own towns. If you're lucky, your contact will have an on-going arrangement with a nearby hotel and offer to make reservations for you. You have nothing to lose by asking, "Say, would you be able to recommend a hotel near your office?"

Your travel agent has a book called *OAG Travel Planner & Hotel/Motel Guide*. This book lists all of the hotels with locations, rates, facilities, and other pertinent facts. By the way, just recently this book has been made available in pocket size. The pocket version is updated quarterly. Your travel agent can also make hotel reservations for you. The travel agent's commission is paid by the hotel. It doesn't cost you anything extra.

You should begin to collect some guides on your own. At the back of each of the in-flight magazines is a BINGO card that invites you to send for information on various items advertised in the magazine. Send for the hotel guides and file them with your travel materials. They contain information on the locations and rates as well as other interesting facts. Most have little maps showing you the exact location. If you belong to AAA, you may request their accommodations guides for every state with maps of major cities. Or you can try the public library's collection of the yellow pages from major cities. Yellow page ads give you a lot of information on the local hotels.

Chains are another answer. Hotel chains and groups exist at all status levels. There are thrifty chains such as the Motel 6 and the Day's End and expensive chains such as the Hilton, Hyatts, Sheratons, and the Raddison group. The idea behind chains is some level of consistency. Holiday Inns, Inc. even uses the theme "no surprises" in advertising its chain of over 1700 inns. They make a big effort to avoid surprises—unpleasant ones, that is.

They have a 33-page training booklet on how to clean a bathroom and they run unscheduled inspections several times each year to see that each of their independent franchises is keeping up to the standards.

Most hotel chains are set up as franchise operations. A local operator ties in with a national franchiser, such as Ramada Inns, Holiday Inn's, Inc., or Best Western in order to ease the advertising and reservations system burden. In fact, easy reservations are an important advantage of dealing with chains. You can call up your local chain member and make reservations in a distant city or use the 800 numbers. One word of caution about 800 numbers. If you are Chicago and call to make a reservation in New York, you may be speaking to someone in Memphis. Don't expect that person to know anything that isn't in the directory.

Making Reservations

A recent ad in *The Wall Street Journal* offered a directory of toll free 800 area code telephone numbers. You don't really need it. To use toll free numbers all you have to do is dial 800/555-1212 and ask the operator for the number for any company you want. If they don't have an 800 number, you will soon find out.

Be prepared when you call for reservations. Know the day, the date, and the time when you plan to arrive, as well as the day and date on which you plan to leave. Tell the reservations clerk if you have any special requirements, such as a king-size bed or a convertible room. Karen is in the executive search business. She does a lot of interviewing in her hotel room. She always orders a king-size bed on the theory that these rooms generally have more furniture and a better floor plan than the standard room.

Have a list of the questions you want to ask. Here are some standard concerns.

- What is the approximate travel time from the airport?
- Is your hotel on the airport limo service route?
- Do you have your own limo service?
- Do you have full room service? What are the hours?
- What are the check-in and check-out times?
- What is my reservation number?

Virginia Lofft, Editor of *Successful Meetings,* adds that when you are making your reservation you should ask if the hotel has special facilities suitable for female business travelers. Many hotels are making special efforts to meet the needs of the female business traveler. The interesting result is that men are happier in those hotels as well. Better lighting, more convenient electrical outlets, more complete room service, and added security measures are welcomed by male travelers. Some hotels have concierge floors that are considerably safer because there is always someone on duty. Other hotels have special "key" service floors where you need a pass key to enter the floor itself. This keeps out non-registered intruders. But if you get a room on one of these key floors, be careful that you're not near the doorway. While the door cuts off the noise of the elevators, there is a lot of noise as the door is opened and latches closed after late night arrivals. Even worse is the nonguest who decides to bang on the door until someone comes to open it.

Some other hotels, Western International among them, have designed special "convertible" rooms. These appear as a living room, but have a concealed pull-down or fold-out bed. You can hold an informal meeting free of the bedroom atmosphere. Ramada Inns have both "Pacesetter Suites," in which a totally separate sleeping room adjoins an executive office-style room, and "Trendsetter Rooms," in which design factors minimize the sleeping area by directing the focus toward the office furnishings instead of the bed.

Most hotels will not hold your reservations past 6:00 PM. If you are going to a low-occupancy city such as Detroit or Atlanta, that may not be a problem. It pays to be cautious anyway since you might just run into a big convention. In cities like New York and San Francisco, where hotels turn people away every night, you could be in trouble. If you think you might be late, the solution is a guaranteed reservation. This means that you promise to pay for the room whether you show up or not. The hotel is protecting itself against no-shows. That's only fair since empty rooms mean lost revenue. You can guarantee your room by giving the clerk your bank card number, your travel and entertainment card number, your company name and address for billing, or by sending a check to cover the first night's charges. The reservation clerk will read back the information and give you a reservation number. Copy it down in your pocket calendar and be prepared to present it if you have any problems when checking in.

Bill Ellis is in the kind of business where he goes back to the same locations time after time after time. His visits last up to a week. He makes a point of stopping in to see the assistant manager at the end of his visit to make a positive comment on the hotel. While he's in the office, he pulls out a $20-dollar bill with a comment like, "Let me contribute this to the fund." It may be the Christmas party fund, the assistant manager's fund, or anything else that person has in mind. Bill says this guarantees him a pleasant reception each time he visits. If your travel involves repeat visits, you will want to become a valued guest.

Checking In

When you present yourself at registration, it is important to establish your professional identity. If you are at a convention, give the name of the group along with your own name. If you are on business, hand the clerk your business card. This also keeps others in the lobby from learning your name. Why is that important? Any nefarious character can get a lot of mileage out of your name. While hotel operators are improving, in many cases they will give out your room number. Then you may find someone pounding on your door or lurking in your hallway. Or a determined person can actually get a key to your room. Busy hotel clerks don't always check ID's when someone steps to the desk and claims he has locked himself out of his room. They ask, "What is that name?" If the name matches the registration, the clerk innocently hands over the spare key.

On Several Occasions She Was Awakened in the Night by Some Drunk Pounding on Her Door and Offering to Pay Her for Personal Services.

But sometimes the clerk isn't so innocent. Ilene is a sales representative for a hospital supplies firm. She travels a sales territory and stays at the same type of commercial level motels as the salesmen. On several occasions she has been awakened in the night by some drunk pounding on her door and offering to pay her for personal services. She used to either ignore it or yell, "GO AWAY!" But even though the door was securely locked, it bothered her that these men knew where she was. Finally one night she asked coyly through the locked door, "Oh, you're so clever. How did you find me?" The answer was that the desk clerk had given out her room number. He was probably expecting a cut. The next morning she reported it to the manager and got the clerk fired. She has also developed a solution that scares off the troublemakers real fast. She simply says in a very loud voice, "Fred, wake up. There's a guy outside the door." The would-be customer has no way to tell if there is or is not a man in the room with her but usually isn't willing to take the chance.

Not all hotel rooms are created equal. Some look out on the park and others look out on garbage containers. Some are large with nice beds and others are so cramped that you can open the door without getting out of bed. Within any hotel there can be great variation. Some of the classic older hotels have added new sections or renovated some floors. Unless the hotel is really crowded, the registration clerk has some discretion in room assignments.

You Need to Make It Clear That You Have High Expectations.

Every hotel has its grade Z rooms located behind the elevator core, next to the vending area or air conditioning system, or in other undesirable situations. You may be better off sleeping in the lobby. Who do you think gets those rooms? Most likely it is the person who looks *least* likely to complain. Since the stereotype of the submissive female is alive and well, you are a prime candidate. You need to make it clear that you have high expectations. One way to do that is to ask questions. Show that you recognize the desirable and the undesirable features in a room. That clerk doesn't want you back at the desk for reprocessing. Here are some things you might want to consider.

The location of the room is important because of safety, convenience, and noise. One of the more dangerous locations is near the stairwell. Bad people know that they can use the stairs to escape. They can lurk in the stairwell waiting to pounce on you as you turn your attention to fitting the key into the doorlock. Virginia Lofft suggests that you ask, "Can you give me a room near but not next to the elevators." This eliminates the need for walks down long, complex corridor systems. Being back to back with the elevator and its *BING BING* can drive you crazy as people arrive at all hours of the night. The same reasoning holds for vending machines and other noise or vibration sources.

In some resort type hotels, the complex includes a main building and several clusters of "outbuildings." The Town and Country Resort in San Diego and the Registry in Phoenix are examples. Both for the sake of safety and convenience, it is desirable to be assigned in or near the main building. If you are in a hotel of this type you should ask, "Do you have a map of the grounds?" Then ask the clerk to show you the location of the room to which you are being assigned. If you don't like it, ask to have your assignment changed before the bellhop loads you into his little golf cart and drives you out to the boonies.

The floor makes a difference, too. Women should avoid ground floor room assignment. Nonguest intruders are more likely to cause problems on the ground floor since the windows provide possible access and escape routes. But it's another trade-off. From a convenience standpoint, the higher you go, the longer you have to wait for the elevators. A trip between the lobby and the twenty-sixth floor during the heavy early morning or pre-dinner traffic periods can take twenty-six minutes.

If, despite your precautions, you are still unhappy with your room assignment, call the front desk and ask for a change. I once checked into a nice hotel in Pasadena at about 8:15 pm. It had been a long day and I was looking forward to curling up in bed with my new book. I quickly unpacked, undressed, washed my face, brushed my teeth, and settled down in bed. Then it started. I had arrived during the band's break. It seems that this hotel had a very popular glass-roofed disco in its courtyard three floors below my window. After 20 minutes I finally decided I couldn't stand it and would have to do something. I called the desk and found that even though it was Thursday, the band played til 1:30 am.

I asked for a different room. The desk clerk wasn't happy and said that I would have to come down to the desk. The thought of redressing wasn't very appealing, and walking through the lobby in my scrubbed face and raincoat didn't seem much better. When I refused, the desk clerk said there was nothing he could do. That didn't make sense to me so I called the operator and asked for the manager. A pleasant explanation was all it took to produce a bellhop with a key for a different and much quieter room.

A Slight Irritation at 8 PM Turns Into Major Aggravation by 3 AM and by That Time Your Options Are Severely Restricted.

If something is bothering you, make the change right away. A slight irritation at 8:00 PM turns into major aggravation by 3 AM and by that time your options are severely restricted. Don't be submissive. If you are presenting yourself in a professional manner, you have a right to be treated with respect. Remember—you're paying the bill.

Hotel Safety

But just because you check into a first class hotel doesn't mean you are safe and secure. You may just have to deal with a little higher class of problems. Melinda reports that in all her travels, the only time she has actually been physically attacked was in the parking garage of a first class hotel in Hartford. The hotel security people were on the spot quickly and were helpful and courteous, but she is still nervous in parking garages.

Rebecca was staying in a nationally known hotel in Los Angeles. She was on her way back from the restaurant about 11:00 PM. The bellman in his fancy red uniform followed her from the lobby keeping up a conversation all the way. Rebecca started out being polite, and then she got concerned. She said things like, "Shouldn't you get back to the lobby in case someone needs you?" and "I'll see you in the morning." Under normal circumstances these are cues that a conversation has ended. Rebecca was playing under the rules of polite social behavior. The bellman wasn't. Rebecca was searching for excuses for his behavior. Perhaps he was concerned for her safety. Maybe he was this friendly with all the guests.

When They Approached Her Room, He Put His Hand Out for Her Key.

When they approached her room, he put his hand out for her key. That is a normal bellman behavior, but not at that time of night. But it wasn't until he offered to give her a massage that Rebecca finally spoke up with a more assertive, "No, thank you. Go back to the lobby since I don't need anymore help from you tonight."

Marian was eating in the hotel dining room in a lovely modern hotel just a block from the Capitol in Washington. She was enjoying her dinner until the waiter started to pay undue attention to her. While she tried to be polite but distant, he finally told her what a great chocolate sundae he made and invited her to join him for a treat when he finished his shift at 11:00 PM. Marina didn't go back, but still regrets that she didn't report it to the management.

Everybody carries around a set of stereotypes. It helps us to sort out our experiences and maintain our balance. Sometimes these stereotypes cause problems. Agnes was checking into a first class hotel in Miami just after noon. She was dressed in a blazer, carrying a briefcase, and handed over a corporate charge card for identification. The clerk apparently couldn't imagine that she was intending to sleep alone. He said, "Are you sure you need to check in right now? The only room I can give you right now only has single beds." Agnes just smiled and answered, "That's alright, there's only one of me."

People are still a little uncomfortable with the idea of a woman staying in a hotel room alone. Of course we sometimes cause our own problems. I was checking out of the Las Vegas Hilton. I had been there three nights and was expecting a bill of about $250.00. The check out lines were quite long. When it was my turn I turned over my key and was handed a bill for about $11.00. Right out loud I said, "Why is this bill so low?" Of course, this got everyone's attention. The clerk said in a low and discreet voice, "Your bill has been paid." I still didn't understand and, not thinking what everyone else was thinking, I continued, "Well, who paid my bill?" The welltrained clerk was still being quiet and discreet and whispered, "I don't know, ma'am, but its been taken care of so you can just leave your key." By this time everyone in line was assuming that I had such complex involvements that I didn't even know who paid the tab for the room. When it suddenly dawned on me how this must look, I was really embarrassed. It turns out that my expenses were being paid by the association holding the convention and had been cleared through a master billing system.

Sandy grew up in Detroit and is very security conscious. On a trip to Minneapolis she stayed in a motel on the outskirts of town. It seemed pleasant enough and was in a nice quiet neighborhood. When she got to her room she did her standard safety check. She latched the security locks on the door and checked the locks on the first floor windows. One of them wouldn't lock. She called the desk and a pleasant young man informed her, "We have never had any problems, so you don't have to worry about the window." She explained that she was happy that that was the case and could understand that he wasn't worried about the windows. Of course, he wasn't the one staying in the room. She insisted that she wouldn't be able to sleep a wink unless he came down to her room and helped her lock the window. Although he didn't like it, he came and locked it.

Shortly After Checking in, One of the Women Went to Open the Draperies and Was Surprised to See a Man Crouching Outside the Window.

You should respect your instincts. Your mind picks up a lot of cues if you will only pay attention. Not long ago there was a story in the newspaper about two women who had gone on a vacation together. To save money they had stayed in a very inexpensive motel. Shortly after checking in, one of the women went to open the draperies and was surprised to see a man crouching outside the window. While it gave her a chill, she allowed her roommate to persuade her that he had probably only dropped something on the walk. Later that night the man broke in, threatened them with a knife, and raped them. When he finally left he said he would be watching and would kill them if they tried to leave the room. Since the cheap motel didn't even have a telephone, they couldn't call for help and were afraid to go out until it got light and other people were around.

It's easy for someone to get in your room. People are careless with keys. They leave them on tables in restaurants, on the checkout counters, and lose them in places where the ill-intentioned can collect them. Some hotels are trying to guard against this with coded keys or locks which can be changed frequently to block out old keys. The problem with the coded keys is that you can't use the key as a reference if you have forgotten your own room number.

Hotel maids can be persuaded to open guest rooms. "Oh, I forgot my key and don't want to go back to the desk. Could you let me in?" is often all it takes to gain entrance. You should never leave anything that is easily stolen in your room. If you have valuable items that you do not wish to carry with you, take them to the front desk where they can be placed in the safety deposit boxes. And remember that you are your most valuable possession. Always chain lock the door when you are in the room—day or night.

While it is really important to use the extra locks on the door whenever you are in the room, be sure to check the room before you lock up. Locks that make it hard to get in also make it hard to get out. Anne Bruce, Editor of *Women's Advocate*, learned this when she worked for Eastern Airlines. One of the flight attendants was alone on a layover in New Jersey. She carefully locked herself in the room only to find a man lurking in the closet. While she ran for the door, he was easily able to keep her from opening it and escaping. After that the flight attendants were taught to hold the door open with a piece of baggage until they had checked the room. Of course, it pays to check the corridor first so that no one is following you in through the propped open door.

If you open a door to a room and feel strange, don't go in. You're not the house detective. Go back to the lobby and ask someone to come with you. If you are embarrassed to admit to your fears, ask them to come up and help you with your bag or to help you tune in the TV.

If the elevator opens and you don't feel comfortable about the person or persons inside, don't get in. The easiest and most graceful way to do this is to exclaim, "Oh, darn, I forgot my book!" and walk away. Even if it looks strange, it is better to embarrass yourself than to get hurt. Elevators are only one of the danger areas in the hotel. Parking garages are terrible places, even in the daytime. Stairwells are equally dangerous. If you see someone loitering in the hallway, turn and walk in the opposite direction. If the person follows, knock on the nearest door and call out a man's name, "Fred, open the door." If the stranger is just heading for the elevator, he won't even notice. If he is a would-be attacker, he isn't going to take the chance on "Fred."

Hotel Etiquette and Procedures

Hotels are in the business of selling rooms. They only have so many to sell. When Conrad Hilton opened his first hotel back before World War I, he and his partner used to sleep in the office so they would have more beds to rent to paying customers. If you decide to stay longer, let the hotel know as soon as possible so that they have a better chance of fitting you into their schedule. If you are leaving early, let them know as a courtesy to other travelers who may now be able to reserve a room.

Hotels also have stated check-out times. Somebody has to decide when a 24-hour day ends. If you find that it is inconvenient to check out on time, call the desk and ask for their policy. Some will allow you a couple of hours grace. Others, especially expensive hotels in high occupancy areas, will charge you by the hour for time beyond the established check-out. If you do not inform the desk clerk, you run the risk of being charged for an extra day. In consideration of other travelers, it is better not to use your room for luggage storage. If you are all packed and ready to go, move your luggage to the lobby where the bell captain will be very happy to check it for you until you are ready to leave.

Brenda Rogers wishes she had moved her bags to the lobby. She was staying in the prestigious Ritz-Carlton hotel in Chicago. The hotel is perched atop the Water Tower Place shopping center, so the lobby is on the twelfth floor. Brenda had an early morning appointment so she packed and left her bags in the room while she went to meet her client. She expected to return to the hotel around 10:30 and have plenty of time to catch a noon flight out of O'Hare.

When she got back to the hotel, it was bedlam. A fire had broken out on the twentieth floor. Brenda's bags were on the 19th floor. She would have left without them, having instructed the hotel to ship the bags to her home, but she was on the first of three stops. She needed her clothes and materials to handle her calls in Dallas and Miami. The elevators were out of the question. Like most, they are heat sensitive and cut off to protect people from being trapped in the elevator shaft.

After a considerable delay, she managed to find a security officer who said that the fire was confined to one room and there was little immediate danger. Together they started up the stairway. By about the sixteenth floor they found water running down the steps and the security officer called it quits. She asked if there was a different stairway. The officer didn't know. Finally, on a hunch, she persuaded him to check with the kitchen staff to see if there was a service stairway. That saved the day. The whole problem could have been avoided by checking out and checking her bags.

In fact, you can usually check out the evening before your departure. All you do is pay your accumulated charges plus one night. If you incur additional charges, the hotel will bill you. If you are checking out of a convention hotel, it is a really good idea to try this. If you check out at noon, you will be waiting in long lines.

Another courtesy in hotel living is to avoid parking your used room service tray in the hall. Other guests really do not want to gaze on your dirty dishes. The room service people appreciate it if you call them when you have finished your meal. This doesn't mean that you have to have anyone in your room to see you with your nightcream and pajamas or lay out a second tip. After placing the call, slip the tray into the hall. They will pick it up there.

It Is Important to Ask in Time to Avoid Crisis.

Most hotel employees do their very best to serve you. Sometimes it is just a matter of knowing who to ask for what. If you don't know, check with the desk. Asking is the key. It seems to be one of the areas where women have an advantage. An amazing proportion of males are reluctant to ask for information. Apparently they are supposed to know all the answers. But it is important to ask in time to avoid crisis. In some places you have to reserve your space on the airport limo in advance. At the Omni in Miami, you must call at least three hours in advance. Hotels on Hotel Circle in San Diego require a one-hour notice. It pays to ask when you check in. Just try to be logical.

One of the common problems of travelers is leaving something behind. I was once at a meeting in San Diego. When I got to my next stop, Los Angeles, I unpacked and found that I didn't have my running shoes and clothes. I called the hotel in San Diego and, having left things behind before, knew to ask for housekeeping. The woman was very helpful and checked the lost and found shelves, but found nothing. She took my home address and telephone number and promised to send the shoes if they showed up. Now it's hard to believe that anyone would walk off with a pair of used running shoes, so they had to be somewhere. Alas, when I got home, I found the shoes beside my bed. I had forgotten to pack them in the first place. Of course, that tells you how consciencious I had been about my running on that trip. Let's hope we are all more consciencious about our on-the-road diets, the topic for the next chapter.

Chapter 6
Thoughts for Food

"An army travels on its stomach."
—Napoleon Bonaparte

"Where did you eat?" seems to be the most common travel question. Food seems to take on increased significance when you are traveling. It's not only that you are working harder and just get hungrier. It has something to do with security. To top it off, dining is a pleasant diversion. Watch the travelogs and they always seem to be talking about food.

Eating Alone

One of the things that both male and female travelers put very high on the "don't like" list is eating alone. "I can handle all the rest of it, but I sure hate eating alone." "Lunch isn't so bad, but eating dinner alone is a killer." The amazing thing is that the most common solution to the problem of eating alone is to order from room service. Women who are assertive in business, self-confident in social interactions, and independent in their actions, still hide out in their rooms and order from the room service menu. At the end of a four day stay, they know the menu by heart.

> **It Isn't the Actual Act of Eating Alone That Bothers People. It's *Being Seen* Eating Alone That Causes the Problems.**

Isn't this still eating alone? Sure, there is the TV for diversion, but it's still eating alone. How about the single person who eats alone at home, but can't stand to do the same on the road? It all points to the conclusion that it isn't the actual act of eating alone that bothers people. It's *being seen* seen eating alone that causes the problem. It's being alone in the same room with others who have company. It's the feeling of being odd and left out. Since we are basically social animals, we just don't seem to be able to adjust to visible isolation. Being isolated in a cubicle of a hotel room is at least invisible isolation. No one but the room service workers see us in our shame.

You can actually get used to eating alone in public and even begin to enjoy it. As Al Borcover, Travel Editor of the *Chicago Tribune*, puts it:

> The terminally timid succumb to room service and the television set in the hotel. Combined, both are a fate much worse than dining out alone. No matter how good room service is alleged to be, and no matter what's on TV, neither will beat the experience of savoring a fine meal alone.

A Matter of Attitude To a great extent, it is a matter of attitude. If you view eating alone as a punishment or an ordeal, it will be just that. If you look at it as an opportunity, you can begin to enjoy it. In fact, there are some substantial advantages to eating alone. For openers, it's much better for your weight control program. You don't have to impress anyone and you can eat whatever you want. Unfortunately, there seems to be a direct relationship between a food's status and its calorie count. Beef Wellington with it's liver pate and pastry has more status and lots more calories than broiled chicken. Anything with sauce has more status than anything without sauce. When you are alone you don't have to eat it if you don't want to. There's no one to talk you into a piece of cheesecake or a chocolate mousse. So what if the waiter has to mask his disapproval. You're paying the bill. And you can eat wherever you want. If you want to go to a coffee shop and eat a low calorie omelette, it's your choice.

But be careful. Be good to yourself. Travel takes a lot of energy, so eating well is important. Eating well doesn't mean eating a lot or spending a lot of money. It means eating higher quality foods prepared in a healthy way. Fast food operations and coffee shops rely heavily on super processed foods and frying. That's okay with moderation. But a steady fast food diet will take its toll. It substitutes unnecessary calories for necessary vitamins.

Eating Alone is Miles Ahead of Eating With a Bore.

Another advantage of eating alone is that you can relax. You aren't on duty. You don't have to entertain anyone with your clever conversation. You don't have to pace your consumption to that of your partner. You can savor your meal. Eating alone is miles ahead of eating with a bore. Look around in any restaurant and you will see at least one woman who is trapped with someone who is a real "empty suit." It isn't worth it. And just think about all that hassle about who gets the check. If you are the only one at the table, it's all yours.

If more women braved the restaurants on their own, it would soon become quite acceptable. Just picture all of those women tucked away in their rooms. We could become a significant economic force in restaurants, just as we have become significant to the airlines and the hotels. There would be tables for one with a good view of the local scenery. There would be special light eater's entrées, like the ones served on United Airlines flights that cater to business travelers. If you are convinced that you are a first class citizen, then you have just as much right to be in that restaurant as anybody else—alone or with companions.

If You Are Convinced That You Are a First Class Citizen, Then You Have Just as Much Right to Be in That Restaurant as Anybody Else.

Don't cheat with a paper or book. If you are going to do that, you might as well stay in your room. This routine says, "I'm nervous about being here. I'm afraid to look you in the eye." And it's insulting to the restaurant's management and the other customers. It's okay in a booth in the coffee shop or at a fast food counter, but dining is as much a social as a physical experience. If the restaurant's management has provided a pleasant atmosphere and well prepared food with good service and if the other patrons are there to enjoy the ambiance, it's "declassée" to be there with your nose stuck in a book.

Single diners, both male and female, are uncomfortable because they don't know what to do to occupy themselves during the moments that are normally devoted to conversation. They feel as if everybody is watching them in their awkwardness. But those other people are having to expend their energies to keep their conversations alive. You, by comparison, have an extraordinary opportunity to observe people. You can try to guess the occupations or, even better, the marital status of others in the restaurant. It's a real kick to watch people pretend to taste the wine. Someday you might really lucky and observe one of those rare instances when someone refuses a bottle. To get the best view, you should politely ask to be seated along the wall. The corner table is best.

Reservations Are Important Borcover recommends choosing the best or one of the best restaurants in town and making a reservation well in advance. You should stick to restaurants that accept reservations. Otherwise you may be subjected to excessive and uncomfortable waiting time in the cocktail lounge.

Bill Schoof, Senior Vice President of Richard D. Irwin, Inc., makes all of his reservations long distance from his own desk at least a week before any business trip. Despite all the technological advances, long distance calls still have a *whoosshing* sound in the background. The restaurant reservations clerks aren't that sophisticated and tend to be impressed with long distance calls. The more assured single female diner can even manage to put the restaurant's personnel on their best behavior by asking, "Do you have any problems with serving a woman who wants to dine alone?" Since they can't admit it even if they do, they are now forced to prove to you that they are pleased to have you there.

In fact, the widespread commotion about the problem of women being treated as second class citizens is grossly exaggerated. And when it does occur, it may well be because the woman invites it. That may be because single people—male and female—skulk into the dining room with all of the body languages that say, "Do what you will with me—I'm a toad. I don't expect to be treated well." If you are pleasantly assertive, if you smile and appear composed and confident, you won't be seated behind the palm or next to the restrooms. Your money is just as green as the guy's at the next table.

> Your Money Is Just as Green as the Guy's at the Next Table.

The Threat of Eating Alone If eating alone has so many advantages, why is it so threatening to so many people? Maybe we feel that others will interpret it as a sign that we are undesirable, that no one wanted to have dinner with us. It can give you the same feeling you had as a teenager when your parents asked if you wanted to go with them to a movie on a Saturday night. It's bad enough not to have a date, but to go to the theater where some of your dated friends might gaze on your disgraceful status —unthinkable! If you are dining alone won't everybody in the restaurant be watching you and thinking, "She looks like a normal person. I wonder why no one likes her?" Or even worse, "I bet she's been stood up."

We all have doubts and insecurities. Our society fosters those doubts. We aren't supposed to feel too good about ourselves. We aren't supposed to kiss ourselves in the mirror. If we should pat ourselves on the back, we might break our arms. We are supposed to slink along the wall and avoid drawing attention to ourselves. We are taught that security is all important. It is a herd animal mentality, the brown paper sack attitude. We are only supposed to do something if a lot of people are doing it with us. There is safety in numbers. That concept sells a lot of soap and toothpaste. "More people use Flash toothpaste than any other leading brand." While you see fans hoisting a "We're number 1!" sign in the stadium, most folks really can't stand the pressure of being "NUMBER ONE."

Most people can't stand the pressure of solitary action. The society calls this "sticking out like a sore thumb," or being "as obvious as a wart on a cow's (behind)." The message is clear: Don't get yourself in the spotlight. Make an effort to blend into the crowd. Don't do anything unique: be a good sheep.

Come on now—where are your manners? You aren't supposed to remind others of their own weaknesses. When someone gazes on you as a single diner and thinks "that poor unloved woman," you must be causing that person the agonizing pain of wondering how she would feel if she were in your place. How inconsiderate of you! You should know better and hide your shame. The alternative might be to embroider your *scarlet D*—for solitary diner— on your breast. Doesn't it sound stupid? That's the point: The whole thing is stupid. You are a self-respecting person and have no reason to apologize to the maitre'd, the waiter, the cab driver, or the dishwasher.

What Other People Choose to Think Is Their Problem, Not Yours.

First of all, eating alone is hardly a sign of rejection. You just happen to be alone, that's all. Second, what other people choose to think is their problem, not yours. If they interpret your aloneness as a sign of rejection, it can only be because they are feeling inadequate and fearful of rejection themselves. It takes a really weak person to gloat over another's misfortune. A comfortable, self-confident person simply sees you as a person who has chosen to dine alone. Third—now brace yourself because this may be a big blow—most people don't care about you anyway. They are far too busy worrying about themselves. Could you describe the people who sat at the next table at lunch yesterday? Do you look up everytime the maitre'd seats someone?

Admittedly, feeling comfortable with eating alone does take practice. It's unfortunate that many professional people shrink from the exercise. Yes, you do get a few sideways glances from others in the room. But surely this problem is never going to go away on its own while professional women hide in their rooms eating off room service trays. Just imagine what the kitchen help thinks when you call in your order. "Hey, Fred, fix up some of the rubber chicken and peas for the old maid up in 1933." The employee who delivers the cart probably reports on you upon returning to the kitchen: "Yeah, it was another one of those broads with the papers all over the bed."

Think of yourself as a pioneer. Look upon it as your responsibility to help to educate restaurant employees. If you appear comfortable and confident, others will readily accept your status. If you slouch into the restaurant and say "You probably don't want to serve me," you will get the reaction you request.

Alone with Company Since both men and women feel uncomfortable eating alone, some people have suggested that hotel dining rooms adopt the practice of the "Captain's Table" where single diners could eat together if they chose. It seems feasible both as a solution for the diners and from an economic viewpoint for the restaurant or hotel. Rather than tying up 12 seats at 6 two-person tables to feed six single people, it would require only one table set for six. The only real problem is timing. The participants would have to arrange to arrive and leave at about the same times. It probably wouldn't be all that difficult for a hotel to post a notice saying, "Dinner at the Captain's Table will be served at 8:00 PM. Join Us." This service could be offered on Sunday through Thursday, the nights when most professional travelers are away from home. In fact, a version of this, "The Solo Table," is being offered at the Ramada O'Hare, a large facility that caters to business travelers.

Until this becomes a widespread practice, there is no reason to eat alone if you don't care to. You can easily invite yourself to eat with another person. As long as you make it clear that you aren't looking for a free meal, most people are delighted. I was seated at a corner table in the dining room in the Tobacco Valley Inn in Hartford, Connecticut. I watched the hostess seat another woman two tables away. This restaurant has a salad bar. I timed it so that we met there and I simply asked, "Would you like to sit with me?" She absolutely leaped at my suggestion. It turned out that this was her first business trip. We had a pleasant meal. One of the reasons for this was that I did all of the listening. Most people love to hear themselves talk. By repeating the last few words each time she paused, I kept her talking all through the dinner hour. I ended up knowing a lot about her. She was in the institutional food business, lived in Chicago, was the youngest of three daughters in an Italian family, and loved gardening. She didn't learn the fisrt thing about me or my business. But she was happy when we said good night. A friend of mine who is in retailing uses these occasions to practice his Walter Mitty routines. He pretends to be something he's not. He claims to be a dentist and gazes into people's mouths. He plays the role of a psychiatrist, an attorney—you name it. It's his escape.

There is quite a nice restaurant complete with fireplace in the Boston airport. I had been standing behind three men at the baggage check-in and then found myself standing behind the same trio at the restaurant reception desk. I commented on our luck at getting to stand in line again and then said, "If you gentlemen aren't going to discuss something confidential, would you mind if I joined you? I'll certainly pay my way, but would enjoy the company." They seemed pleased. We had a very nice time talking about our business activities and then departed for four different cities.

What You Do Is Up to You and Most Other People Really Don't Care.

The point is that you can choose to be alone or you can choose to be with people. What you do is up to you and most other people really don't care. Now, don't misunderstand, room service has its place. If you are in the mood to eat a quiet dinner alone in your room because you are tired, have washed your hair, have work to do, or are waiting for a phone call, you don't have to be ashamed. But if you are hiding there, you're cheating yourself. You should take a chance on the outside world once in a while. You may learn to like it. If you want a dinner partner, they are available without cost and without risk. You simply have to ask. When you are traveling, you can step outside normally accepted behaviors with little risk. If someone should reject your invitation, you are none the worse for the experience. As long as you are doing what you want to do and feel comfortable with your actions, the rest of the world will learn to live with it.

Selecting Restaurants

Every major city has its "restaurants," the well-known, expensive, five-star-rated name places. In New Orleans you can go to Brennans, Galatoire's, Commander's Palace, The Court of Three Sisters, Antoines, and many others. In San Francisco the "places" are Vanessi's, Scoma's, La Bourgogne, and Sam's Grill and Tadich's Grill. In New York there are many famous places including the "Windows on the World" on the 108th floor of World Trade Center, Four Seasons, Twenty-One, and Sardi's in the theater district. In Memphis it's Justine's. In Atlanta it's Nicoli's Roof. In Chicago there are many famous places including The Whitehall Club, Nick's Fishmarket, and Sages East.

But those are the big name fancy spots where dining is an event. How do you find a place that will serve you a reasonable meal in a reasonable atmosphere at a reasonable price within a reasonable time frame? Wandering around the streets seems too chancy. You're going to need some information. There are three really good sources. First, there is the yellow pages right in the desk drawer in your hotel room. Along with lots of other useful information for a stranger in town, it has a complete listing of the choices classified by type of food. In larger cities, the restaurants are reclassified by location. A little reserach there should narrow it down to four or five possibilities. The next step is either to ask your local contacts or hotel employees for comments on the places on your list. Always ask more than one person.

Unfortunately, food is a high status value topic. A good indication of that is that a lot of people turn up their noses when you mention McDonald's, but they have still sold billions of hamburgers. Either somebody is eating a lot of hamburgers or the rest are sneaking in late at night. Everybody seems to pretend that they only eat at first class places, but there are lots of successful less-than-classy restaurants.

You Have to Be Careful That You Don't Ask in Such a Way as to Impress Your Source Rather Than Get the Information You Need.

So when you ask for advice you have to be very careful that you don't invite information that is intended to impress you. You have to be careful that you don't ask in such a way as to impress your source rather than get the information you need. Describe the kind of place you would prefer. What are you going to gain by impressing the bell captain, the cab driver, or a stranger on the plane?

Give people your price preferences: "I don't want to spend much more than $15.00." Tell them the kind of atmosphere you want: "I'd prefer someplace where I can see what I'm eating." Let them know about your time constraints: "I'd like to be able to get back to the hotel before 9:00." Tell them how far you want to travel: "I don't have a car here so I'd prefer that it be within a couple of miles of the hotel." Tell them what kind of food you like: "I want something fairly light. I ate lunch late." The more specific you are, the more likely it is that the person will be able to give you the information you need.

You will find it worthwhile to do some research before you get to your destination. Mobil's Restaurant Guide is only one of many fine listings of restaurants. The in-flight magazines offer regular reviews of restaurants in cities serviced by the sponsoring airlines. Malcolm Forbes rates restaurants in *Forbes* by using a neat system based on the traffic light. A green spot means that you should make an effort to go. Yellow means it's alright. And guess what a red spot means? Most hotel rooms have a city magazine that lists restaurants. Some of these are amazingly descriptive. The reviewers pride themselves on their independence. You should, of course, always consider who is buttering who's bread. You might talk to people in the plane. Flight crews are usually very helpful.

One of the thrills of traveling is sampling the area's special food. If you are in Boston, you should be trying the seafood. In Kansas City or Chicago, the specialty is beef. In Dallas you shouldn't miss out on Big Red's Barbecue with its barbecued beef and hush puppies. In Milwaukee you should give the weinerschnitzel a try. In Louisiana it's red beans and rice, and in Florida you will have a chance to finish off with a slice of peanut butter streusel or key lime pie.

Battling Calories

Travel can be very hard on your figure. People have been known to take that return flight with unbuttoned buttons and unzipped zippers. It is more difficult to control your diet on the road and it's lots easier to snack and drink. There may not be a restaurant in the country that serves breakfast without hash brown potatoes and toast dripping in butter—they spread it on with a brush. The jelly is right there on the plate. How many people eat hash browns for breakfast at home? A bowl of cold cereal is an effort. At lunch time your sandwich is served with chips that you wouldn't eat at home. But, heck, you've paid for them and they'll only go in the trash. Someplace in the world people are starving.

Those Calories Count the Same on the Road as They Do at Home.

That cocktail on the plane or after the meeting won't help much. Liquor holds a lot of empty calories. And then at dinner there are rolls and butter, special sauces, fried foods you wouldn't bother to fix at home, and even almonds on your broiled fish. There are lots of ways for extra calories to creep into your daily diet on the road. Believe it or not, those calories count the same on the road as they do at home. If the trip is long enough you can grow out of your clothes before you get home. The solution is *not* to start off with clothes a size too large.

The solution is a combination of discipline and self-confidence. Any restaurant that can serve eggs with hash browns and toast, can serve plain eggs. If you can't order a side order, order the complete breakfast and insist that they bring only the eggs. Be willing to pay for the hash browns and toast that weren't served. If the cook sends you a plate with all the trimmings, send it back.

Perrier is a boon to the traveler. Ordering a club soda has no zip whatsoever, but a "Perrier with lime" smacks of class. The surgeon general would turn blue in the face issuing letters of commendation to the restaurants and hotels that protect their patrons from saccharrin in the form of diet sodas. Illegal substances are more readily available. But the marketing efforts of the mineral water people have at least made that option much more available.

Since dinner is usually the hardest, try to stick to a salad for lunch. But beware of salad dressing. You can eat lettuce til it sticks out your ears with no problems, but three tablespoons of salad dressing is your total luncheon calories allotment. Restaurants tend to be overly generous with salad dressings. Always ask for the dressing on the side and ladle it out sparingly. It is even better to skip the dressing and ask for a wedge of lemon instead. Besides, that's one way to judge a restaurant. The really high class restaurants conceal their lemon wedges in little gauze wrappers tied with a green ribbon.

Dinner calories are concentrated in the entrées and the desserts. Did you know that most full service restaurants will prepare a vegetarian plate if you request it, even if it isn't on the menu? And since they charge about the same price for the less costly vegetarian plate as they do for a standard entrée, they tend to put quite a bit of effort into it. A vegetarian plate one night will leave you free of guilt the next night.

Another trick is skip the entrée column entirely and order a double appetizer. If you order escargot dripping in garlic butter this isn't going to help. It surely tastes good though. But a double shrimp cocktail is a pleasant and light dinner. Remember, you are paying the bill. Without people like you, the restaurant would have to close its doors for good. You must expect to pay for good food and good service, but you also have a right to get what you pay for. If you don't want ground pepper on your salad, it's your choice. And if you want to drink white wine with your steak, it's up to you.

Handling the Menu

Dining can be a lot more pleasant if you know what you are ordering. Some restaurants seem to go out of the way to make their menus elegant but uninformative. It's assumed that the sophisticated diner knows the meanings of various terms. Here is a short course on some of the more commonly encountered menu terms.

Appetizers
Anchois	anchovies
Champignons	mushrooms
Crudites	raw vegetables
Escargot	snails
Fruits de mer	clams, oysters
Pate de:	slices of meat/fowl loaf of
foie gras	goose or duck liver
campagne/pays	pork
foie de volaille	chicken liver

Sauces
A la perigourdine	truffles/foie gras
Bernaise	herbs/wine/egg yolk
Chasseur	wine/mushrooms/shallots
Fondue	cheese/wine
Hollandaise	egg yolk/butter/lemon juice
Mornay	white sauce/cheese
Newburg	cream/butter/sherry/egg yolk
Remoulade	mayonnaise/herbs (chilled)
Vinaigrette	oil/vinegar

Meats
Bifteck	steak
Chateaubriand	large thick steak (for two)
Chevreuil	venison
Jambon	ham
Tournedo	small thick steak
Veau	veal

Fish and Fowl
Anguille	eel
Coquilles St. Jacques	scallops
Coq/Pollo	chicken
Crevettes	tiny shrimp
Scampi	large shrimp
Grenouilles	frogs' legs
Homard	lobster
Huitres	oysters
Truite	trout

Vegetables
Pilaf	rice cooked in broth
Pommes de terre	potato
au four	baked
mousseline	mashed
Ratatouille	casserole of eggplant/tomatoes/onions/peppers/zucchini

General Terms
A la carte	priced individually
Almondine/amandine	with slivered almonds
Au beurre/Meuniere	in butter
Au gratin	with cheese
Au jus	in natural juices
Au lait	with milk
Au poivre	with pepper
Au riz	with rice
Au vin	in wine
Du jour	special of the day
En croute	baked in pastry or crust
Farcie	filled or stuffed
Flambe	set aflame before serving
Florentine	with spinach
Glaceed	candied or glazed
Jardiniere	with mixed fresh vegetables
Julienne	cut in thin strips
Lyonnaise	with onions
Montmorency	served with cherries
Mousse	mixed with whipped cream
Nicoise	with tomatoes and garlic
Provencale	with garlic
Risolle/Sauteed	fried
Scallopini	thin slices of sauteed meat
Smitane	with sour cream
St. Germain	with peas

Dining Unalone

Everyone seems to worry about dining alone, but dining with others can present problems as well. The ones that get the most press are the problems faced by a woman when she is entertaining a man. "How can I make sure I get the wine list and the check?

Who should taste the wine? Will he be embarrassed when I pay the check?" Things are improving dramatically.

In recognition of the growing number of professional women, many restaurants are now training their employees to be more alert to noncouple situations. If there is any doubt as to who is "hosting" the meal, the check is to be placed equi-distant from the diners. While this is much better than automatically presenting it to the male, it still leaves that awkward pause until one of you reaches for the check.

Handling the Check When there were fewer women paying the check, one of the suggested ploys was to arrange prepayment or direct billing with the restaurant prior to arriving with your guest. Just think of the impact of that. First, there is no natural conclusion to the dinner. The standard script is that you get the check, pay the check, leave a tip, ask your dinner partner "Are we ready?" and then leave the restaurant. If no check arrives, there is no cue to leave. Beyond that, it leaves your guest a bit concerned that you are both going to be arrested for skipping out without paying the bill.

This Procedure Gives Off a Very Unpleasant Underlying Message.

The worst part is that this procedure gives off a very unpleasant underlying message. It says, "Dear dinner partner: I was afraid that you lacked the sophistication and the maturity to handle this situation, so I felt I had to take actions to relieve you of the reponsibility." It's patronizing.

Another caution that was offered was that you pay with a charge card instead of cash. The supposition was that a charge card was less threatening. Again, that puts your guest in a childlike position. Why would you want to go to dinner with anyone who can't understand that a charge card means money? Of course, charge cards do have their advantages. You don't have to count out bills. You never run out of money. And some charge cards have a status impact. If you are carrying a Carte Blanche, Diner's Club, or an American Express Card (especially the gold card) it identifies you as a woman who is accustomed to handling financial transactions.

The best course is to make it clear at the outset that you

intend to pay for the meal. There are a lot of simple and comfortable ways to do this. If this is a friend or a more enlightened person you can say, "Hey, let's go to dinner tonight. I'll treat." Another easily accepted idea is, "Look, I'll buy dinner tonight and you can get the check next time." Even if there never is a next time, you have preserved your guest's sense of dignity and worth. If you do feel that the person might be less-than-comfortable with the idea of a woman buying his dinner, you can use, "Say, I'm on an expense account. How about letting my company buy our dinner?" You can say that even if it isn't true.

If you have ended up at the dinner hour together and it isn't clear who asked whom, someone is going to have to speak up. You can work a trade-off. Make a suggestion like, "Gee, if you'll get the cabs, I'll buy the dinner." If you are in the cocktail lounge you can suggest, "Why don't you get this check, and I'll pop for dinner."

Then, to avoid that awkward moment when the check arrives at the table, you should try to be alert that the check is coming. Reach out and say, "I'll take that," before it hits the table. That means that you should always choose the seat that gives you the best view of approaching service. Since etiquette still dictates that you, the woman, should follow the maitre'd to the table, you have the first choice of seats. Look around as you walk to the table. Try to figure out where you should sit so that you can observe the action. Now, the maitre'd will attempt to seat you in the low control seat. It's the seat with your back to the action. Rather than taking the offered chair, simply say, "I think I'd prefer to sit on the other side of the table."

Is This a Dinner or a Date? One of the problems with dining unalone is that so much of the restaurant atmosphere and the after working hours time cycle stimulates male/female date-like feelings and behaviors. Do you remember the classic sensuous eating scene in the movie *Tom Jones*? There are candles, couples, music, and wine. The environment pushes all the buttons that can bring otherwise normal sensible people to the brink of unsensible behaviors. Even if that isn't what you have in mind, it can be misinterpreted. During a relaxed dinner the conversation can easily turn to more personal topics. There is only one answer. Know what you want and where you are going before you go to dinner. Be in control of yourself. Any idea that didn't look good at 5:00 PM hasn't improved any by midnight.

Any Idea That Didn't Look Good at 5:00 PM Hasn't Improved Any by Midnight.

You have to eat something someplace. So why not make it a pleasant experience. Good food in a pleasant atmosphere can be one of the things you do for yourself while you are traveling. All it takes is a little planning and a little self-confidence.

Chapter 7
Money Matters

Sex and money have been nominated as the two most important forces that make the world go around. There may be other contenders, but these two would surely get a lot of votes. And money might even be the winner. People who are fairly easy going on most subjects can get very up-tight when it comes to money. Folks will talk about some of the most intimate details of their lives, but clam up when it comes to revealing the numbers on their paychecks. Money is a touchy topic.

Most stay-in-the-office workers can get through the normal work day with about one financial transaction, and that's only if they eat lunch out. When you are traveling, you get to handle a lot of money and money substitutes on an average day. You may be reaching for your money or charge cards a dozen times each day. Money matters can be a big source of concern.

As your supply of cash dwindles you begin to wonder, "Will I have enough?" At the restaurant the question is, "Was that a big enough tip?" You listen to the meter ticking while the cab sits in rush hour traffic and fret, "How much is this going to cost me?" You are relaxing in a cocktail lounge with a person you just met and the drinks arrive. He gets his money out first. You suddenly think, "Am I getting myself obligated?" To put it bluntly, money matters!

Money Attitudes

Traveling will give you lots of practice in handling money. The way you handle money depends a lot on your money attitudes.

Anne Bruce, Editor of *Women's Advocate*, admits how important it is to her to be in control in a situation. She knows that picking up the check gives her the control she needs. There is a tremendous amount of self-confidence to be gained from paying or at least knowing that you are willing and able to pay your own way. Just think of it: How much can it cost to pick up the tab? If you took someone out to lunch every single working day and you always paid the check, it would cost you around $3000 a year. For that you would have 250 people who "owed you." That's a pretty good investment in itself, but it's even better when you realize that you could have ended up "owing" 250 people.

Why are we embarrassed by money? Part of it might be that an undue concern about money might be interpreted as a sign that we are either cheap or poor. Most of us wouldn't care to have either of these labels. But financially confident people have little fear of this concern. Midas Muffler ran an ad about "ol' man Purdy" who still drives his ancient car and cashes in on their lifetime guarantee. When the attendent questions his concern about his money, Ol' man Purdy responds, "How do you think I got this rich?"

A successful New York businessman was complaining because he had gotten caught in a very common trap. He had given a newstand attendant a $20-bill and made the mistake of looking away while the attendant made change. The clerk slipped the $20.00 in his pocket and gave back change for a $10.00 Most of the time, this little scam comes off without a wrinkle. The customer accepts the change without even noticing the switch.

When our friend complained, the clerk conscientiously searched his stack of tens and declared that no mistake had been made. How could this man complain about the measley $10.00. As he stood there in his $300 suit casually chatting about multi-million-dollar corporations, he knew—everyone around him knew, and he knew that everyone around him knew—that the $10.00 itself didn't mean anything to him—it was the principle. If $10.00 looked like a real loss to him, he might have been afraid to broadcast his story for fear that others would see him as poor or cheap.

Con artists and petty thieves prey on those who look like easy marks. Travelers qualify because they are generally in a hurry and less likely to cause problems since they'll be in another city before they realize that they've been cheated. The organized bands of money grabbers in the airports are always on the lookout for anyone who appears weak or confused. They force a flower, a book, or a candy cane on you and then use all their skills to make you feel cheap if you don't give "just a little" to help their cause, which may range from animal protection to drug rehabilitation to the love of God. Don't even be polite. These people are leeches. No respectable organization raises funds by attacking people in an airport. Your best defense is a glaring look and a firm, "Don't you touch me!"

> **No Respectable Organization Raises Funds by Attacking People in an Airport.**

Thrifty or Cheap? A lot of women just aren't used to the give and take in money matters. They aren't used to paying someone else's bills. If you are over 30, you grew up during the period when the boys paid for the movies and the pizzas. You were never even expected to pay for yourself, let alone pay for someone else. And it hasn't changed as much as we might like to think. Picture all of the restaurant and cocktail lounge checks that will be written tonight. What percentage of those checks will be paid by men?

You've seen the routine when three matrons go out to lunch: "Who had the crab salad?" "I didn't order any coffee." "Let's see now, yours is $4.75 and Mary's is $3.95." It's pathetic. These women have never learned the give and take. "You buy this round and I'll get the next." And sometimes it is all give. Sometimes you get caught paying the check and someone else ducks out. Just ask yourself who pays in the end. Cheapness is its own reward.

> **Cheapness Is Its Own Reward.**

A very successful businessman and traditional gentleman was at a conference. He invited a group of men to dinner. Since there were nine people in the party, they took two cabs. To be polite, he and his wife split up. When the two cabs arrived at the restaurant, he paid his driver and walked back to escort his wife from the second cab. There he found four men standing with their hands in their "deep pockets" while his wife was digging into her evening bag for money to pay the cabbie. He was so offended that he cancelled the dinner plans on the spot. The cab fare was under $5.00. Cheapness is its own reward.

Explaining Spending Behaviors Look at the factors that contribute to tight fists and deep pockets. The more money you have, the easier it is to be a free spender. Women typically do not earn as much money and therefore tend to be more careful with what they have. Despite all the brouhaha about equal opportunity, recent statistics show that women still earn less than 60 cents for each dollar earned by a man. And an even more disturbing statistic is that a woman with a college degree will earn less over her lifetime than a male high school drop-out.

Spending behavior is also related to the way you receive your money. If you are paid on a commission basis, you can always go out and hustle more business to cover your expenditures. The average woman is paid on a salary or a time-related basis. She is paid so much per week or per year. That's all there is. That number is going to stay the same until she gets a merit raise, a cost of living raise, or changes jobs. Her income figure is fixed and predictable. There isn't anything that she can do to change it within the forseeable future.

Her task, of course, is to maintain the most gratifying lifestyle possible given the income limitation. The only way she can do that is to save money. It becomes an exercise in living within a budget by doing without, doing with less, or substituting time and energy for money. The reasoning goes like this: "I guess I can wait til next winter for that new coat," or "If I do without cleaning help, I can get that new coat this winter," or "Whoopee! I found it on sale. I really wanted a navy one, but the brown one is okay."

These patterns have been going on for generations: Men went out and earned money—never quite enough—and women were supposed to figure out ways to stretch it. We are still trying to figure out ways to stretch those dollars. Just look at the practical tips suggested in most of the women's magazines or newspapers: "A penny saved is a penny earned." The amount of time or energy you put into saving those pennies doesn't seem to matter. They tell you how you can turn $3.00 worth of materials into $30.00 worth of something else in ten easy steps. The kicker is that it will take you 30 hours. According to the columnist you have saved $27.00. In reality you have worked for less than a dollar an hour. But that's okay, since your time isn't worth anything anyway. Now, there is nothing wrong with being fiscally responsible. Throwing money away isn't the objective. People who overspend risk being criticized for ignorance, insecurity, or buying their friends. But remember that your time, your peace of mind, and your ego have value—more value than your money or your physical possessions. The objective is to achieve a reasonable balance between the value of your money and your self-value.

Traveling will give you a great deal of concentrated experience in handling money matters. The areas that seem to cause the greatest concern are tipping, mechanics of money handling, expense accounts and reimbursements, and the efficient use of money or, in other words, not wasting money.

Tipping

The term *tips* supposedly originated when some English pub-keeper placed an old jar on the bar with the sign, "To Insure Prompt Service." That's what tips are supposed to be. They are supposed to serve as an incentive for various service industry employees to keep up a high level of effort in the face of all the aggravation that comes from dealing with the public.

Women as a group have the reputation of being poor tippers. As a result, women are sometimes the victims of poor service. Anyone who has worked in a tip-based industry knows that there is a strong dependence on stereotypes. It's only human. You try to figure out who might be the best tipper and then concentrate your efforts on good service for that person. If they seat the single woman diner by the door to the kitchen or the restrooms while the single male diner may get better treatment, it's because he is expected to be a good tipper unless he proves otherwise. She is being judged guilty until proven innocent. But you don't get to lay your tip on the table before the meal or wear a sign that reads "GENEROUS TIPPER." It's a vicious circle.

You Don't Get to Lay Your Tip on the Table Before the Meal or Wear a Sign that Reads "Generous Tipper."

The stereotype of the woman as a poor tipper has some merit. It has something to do with history and virtue. It's nothing new. Traditionally men have had more bravado while women have worried about stability. My uncle was the editor of a Hearst newspaper during the "Golden Years." Publishing isn't the highest paid industry and he had three young children to support. His wife resented it when he left a big tip "to show off." Sometimes she would lag behind and pocket a part of the tip.

Some people object to tipping as a poor way to handle the compensation of employees. They argue that the hotel or restaurant should pay the people more and forget the tips. But let's be logical. The hotel or restaurant would simply add the cost to your bill anyway. You would still be paying and you wouldn't have any meaningful way to express your level of satisfaction. Tipping is one way of showing service people that you appreciate their efforts on your behalf. Most service people are trying hard to do what they are supposed to do. It always pays to treat them with respect and consideration.

If you are going to travel, you are going to get to pay the piper. Our objective here is to define the best and the right way to do that. There is a right way. There are four possible errors: overtipping, undertipping, tipping when you shouldn't, and not tipping when you should. So, who should be tipped and how much? Tips are customary in hotels and restaurants and lounges, cabs, and for skycaps in airports.

Airports   Never tip an airline employee either in the air or on the ground. They are not allowed to accept tips and it will only embarrass both of you. But do tip the skycap who checks your luggage on your way in or helps you with your luggage on the way out. Fifty-cents per bag or a one dollar bill is standard. If you don't tip him when he checks your luggage, it may never get there. Some people complain that the curbside check-in tip is a version of protection money. But sometimes this skycap saves you from yourself.

At the end of a two-week trip, I was checking in at LAX and as I handed the skycap my bag I said, "Please check this on the 5:30 PSA flight to Sacramento." He said, "There's no such flight." I was determined. After all, I live in Sacramento and I knew I was going home. He insisted, so I dug out my ticket and found that I was flying to San Francisco. Then I remembered that I had driven to San Francisco to meet with some people before making the trip south to Los Angeles. I smiled and thanked the skycap as I handed him a dollar. I could still be wandering around the Sacramento airport parking lot looking for my car as it sat parked at the San Francisco airport.

Cab Drivers   The standards for tipping cab drivers are 15 percent of the fare, with about a 30-cent minimum. You should throw in an extra quarter or 50 cents for the cab driver who handles your luggage. If the driver volunteers to wait for you in a remote location and does not leave the meter running, an extra dollar is reasonable.

Hotels In hotels the tippable employees are the doorman, the bellhops, the room service person, and the maid. When should you tip and how much should you give? You should tip the doorman as he deposits your luggage at the registration desk. While 50 cents would do, it's a lot neater and easier to hand over a folded dollar bill. Be sure to deliver it with a smile and a "thank you." The minimum for the bellhop who carries your bag to your room is 50 cents per bag. If your bag could pass as a steamer trunk, you may want to offer a bigger tip, but in most cases that dollar bill will cover you nicely. Wait until he has opened the door, deposited your bag on the stand, checked the lights, draperies, bath, or whatever. Position yourself near the door and hand him the tip as he comes back past you.

You should tip any employee who comes to your room to do something for you at your request. If you call the desk and ask to have an iron or a hair dryer and it is delivered by the bellman, it's another dollar. The bellman is also the person who delivers your drycleaning. Generally you do not tip when the cleaning is picked up, but you do tip when it is delivered. If you are in the room, peel off another one-dollar bill. If you aren't in the room, it would be considerate to stop by the bell captain's station later in the day and drop off a tip "for the person who delivered my drycleaning."

Policies for room service vary. In some cases a service charge is added to the bill. If you aren't sure whether or not to tip, just ask. "Did they take care of you on this?" Now room service tips do not necessarily follow the standard 15 percent rule of normal restaurant service. If you only ordered a bucket of ice, 15 percent of nothing would be nothing. Again, 50 cents is the minimum while the dollar is more common.

Tipping the maid seems to be the most questionable practice. In Europe it is the prevailing custom. Here it is more optional. If you ask for some special service, you should leave a tip. For example, if you take a nap and ask to have your bed made up a second time late in the afternoon, a tip is justified. The recommended amount is 50 cents to $1.00 per night. Be sure to leave it where the maid will find it and know that it is intended as a tip. To put it on the desk with a little note that says "thank you" solves that problem.

I was staying at the Hyatt Regency in New Orleans. As I sat in a meeting, I scratched my ear and realized that I had left my earrings in the room. I remembered laying the tiny gold chains on the flowered bedspread while I went to answer the phone. "Well, dummy, there goes another $45." I went back to my room at lunchtime on the outside chance that the maid had not yet gotten to my room. Surely the tiny earrings would have been lost in the process of changing the sheets. She had been there all right. But much to my surprise, there on a sheet of paper on the desk were my tiny earrings. She could have lost them or even taken them. What could I have said? I left a $5.00 tip. I also told my story to the assistant manager when I checked out. Honest service should be rewarded.

Restaurants and Lounges In restaurants there are four potential tipping points. If you have a drink in the cocktail lounge prior to being seated, you should tip the cocktail waitress. In some restaurants you will settle the bar bill before going to the dining room. If so, simply add the standard 15 percent to the bill. Other restaurants will add your bar bill to the dinner check. When they call you for your table, ask "Do I settle this with you or does it go on my dinner check?" If it goes on the dinner check, estimate the bar bill and leave a 10-20 percent tip on the table.

The next stop is the maitre'd. Whether or not you tip the person who seats you depends on the service you have requested. If you arrive without a reservation, a tip might get you in. If you bring extra people or in any way cause the maitre'd to make adjustments to accommodate you, a tip is in order. These tips are delivered at the maitre'd's stand prior to seating. the amount might range from a dollar to $10.00 depending on the situation.

If you are in a first class restaurant with a wine steward, the authorities recommend tipping him 10 percent of the cost of the wine at the time that he opens the bottle at the table. Having been to a lot of restaurants, I have never done this nor have I ever seen it done. I suppose you might do this if you requested very special service. It just seems awkward to be digging out your cash at the moment when you might be proposing a toast. It is more common to include that tip next to the waiter's tip at the end of the meal. If you are paying with a charge card, you should write in the wine steward's tip separately and comment, "I included a tip for the wine steward." If you are paying cash, hand the waiter a separate bill and say, "This is for the wine steward."

Restaurant employees work in teams. The waiters and waitresses realize that they will make more money if the tables in their areas are reset rapidly and quietly. They know that people want their water glasses filled and their places cleared promptly. They give a part of their tips to the busboys To Insure Prompt Service. They realize that the customers evaluate the entire dining experience when they leave tips. They will deliver your tip to the wine steward. They want things to continue to go smoothly in the future.

Tip the waiter or waitress from 10 to 20 percent of the pretax total. Don't be embarrassed to figure it out. If you are charging the bill, you even have a pen to work with. If you are doing it in your head, start by figuring 10 percent of the pretax total. That's easy. Ten percent of $23.00 is $2.30. Ten percent of $55.00 is $5.50. Then either add nothing more if service was not too good, half again as much if service was okay, or double it if service was super. It's not hard to add $1.15 to $2.30, or $2.75 to $5.50. If you try to multiply $55.00 by .15 you'll get much more confused.

Money Mechanics

There are four basic ways to handle traveling expenses: cash, plastic, traveler's checks, and direct billing. Each has its place. Deciding which to use where depends on cost, security, image, availability, acceptability, and personal preference. Here are some of the things you will want to take into consideration.

Cash You need cash for tips, for ground transportation, some of your meals, drinks, tolls and parking fees, phone calls, and miscellaneous items like newspapers. Cash is always acceptable. One of the big drains on any cash reserve is cab fares. My all time one day high was $98.00 in Houston. On another day I spend $46.00 within an hour tripping back and forth to appointments close to O'Hare airport. Right now only one cab district in the United States accepts charge cards. The rest expect cash money.

One big question is how much cash to carry when you travel. No one wants to be stranded without cash. Can you imagine getting back to your home airport without enough cash to bail your car out of the parking lot? But carrying large amounts of cash is dangerous. The answer depends on your attitude toward cash, your expected activities, and your reimbursement situation. Try to estimate your daily expenditures and then multiply that amount by the number of days you will be traveling. Don't judge it by the amount of cash that flows through your hands at home. You will need lots more. If you will be paying cash for your meals, it's quite normal to go through at least $50.00 a day. If you are headed for a high cost city like New York or San Francisco, tack on a safety margin of at least 15 percent. Barbara Jenkins recommends starting off with an extra $50.00 in one-dollar bills for tips. "It's so easy to peel one off and be on your way."

If you are traveling internationally, you can get a $10.00 "starter kit" of currency from your local bank to handle tips on arrival, but will want to make substantive currency conversions at a bank at your destination. Watch the conversion rates carefully since the daily fluctuations can make a lot of difference. You can get this information by calling the bank.

Get Yourself a Money Clip

Here's another tip: Get yourself a money clip. As Barbara says, "I've learned a lot from men who travel. They do a lot of things just because it works out better that way." Most men carry their money in a money clip in their right hand trouser pocket. The clip provides the weight to keep the money from inching it's way out of the pocket as you sit down. The advantage is that your money is readily available. You can have your money out as fast as that man across the table. It really alters the power relationships. Even if you end up letting someone else pay, visible green dollar bills make it clear that you intend to be in control of yourself. It's awkward to be digging in your briefcase or wallet to get out a tip. I carry enough money for the day in my money clip and keep the rest in my wallet. Of course, to make this work, you have to be careful to buy skirts with side pockets. And you may want to request a simple and invisible alteration to make the pocket deeper. Besides the money clip, I always tuck an extra $20-bill in the pocket of my briefcase. If my wallet was lost or stolen, I'd still have enough to get help.

If you need more money, there are several places to get it. If you belong to one of the airline clubs, you can cash a check for $50-$100 at any airline ticket counter. You can usually cash a check for up to $50.00 at your hotel. Even if you don't take your checkbook, it's a good idea to carry a few personal checks in your wallet for emergencies. If you travel a lot, you may want to do some of your banking with the most well known bank in your area.

If you get in serious money problems in a foreign country, you can go to the American Embassy where you can get the money to get home. They will not be able to give you money to continue your trip. One way to get money to another country is through airline tickets. If someone back home will arrange to buy you a ticket, you can go to the airport wherever you are and pick up that prepaid ticket. You can then cash it in and use the money. Some charge card guarantee plans will advance you $50.00 and buy you a one-way ticket home if your wallet and credit cards are stolen. You must be able to come up with your identification number, however. Take all of your charge cards and your drivers license and your insurance cards and lay them face down on the copy machine and run off several copies. Tape one in your suitcase and leave one at home.

Traveler's Checks Traveler's Checks are a compromise between cash and credit cards or personal checks. You have paid for the checks already, so whoever cashes them for you need not worry about collecting from you. The checks will be redeemed by the traveler's check company. To make the checks the most cashable, you want to buy them in fairly small denominations. It means that you have to sign your name a few more times. But if you hand the cashier a $50.00 traveler's check to pay for your $2.00 magazine, you may meet with resistance.

There are several brands of traveler's checks. Are they worth the fee? The principal selling point is that they can be replaced if they are lost or stolen. It is a good idea to keep one record of the serial numbers separate from the checks in your suitcase or your coat pocket. You should also keep a copy of that record at home just in case you lose everything. If you lose your traveler's checks, you must be able to report these numbers to get them replaced.

Charge Cards How do you decide when to charge and when to pay cash? If you don't have a cash advance from your employer and will have to fill out an expense account, charge everything you can. It makes it so much easier. Charging provides a nice record of your expenditures. If you do have a cash advance—and be sure to check if this is possible, since it's better to use someone else's money whenever possible—you may want to pay some bills, usually meals, in cash. You certainly don't want to turn your cash advance back in after the trip and then hope that the reimbursement check gets to you before your charge account bills come due. And using cash does help you to visualize your expenditures. It's so easy to sign that charge form without thinking about the numbers. Then when your monthly statement comes, it can be a real shock.

If you will be renting a car, you will have to charge it. Without a charge card and a valid driver's license, you cannot rent a car. They couldn't care less about cash. Even if you agreed to prepay the rental fees, you could run off with the car. Of course, in many cities you need cash for gas.

There are two kinds of charge cards: the Travel and Entertainment cards—American Express, Carte Blance, and Diner's Club—and then the bank cards—Visa and MasterCard. The bank cards tend to carry fewer status points, since traditionally there have been no membership or initiation fees. Bank cards are credit cards. That means that you may choose to pay only a part of the amount due and the bank will extend you credit on the balance. In fact, it is the anticipated interest revenues on the credit that have allowed banks to offer these cards with no fees. However, as increasing costs of lending money squeeze the profits out of the credit business, more banks have been initiating yearly fees or transactions charges on the use of their credit cards. The T&E accounts are fully payable each billing period. But status isn't the only issue. You must also consider the acceptability of each type of card and the benefits offered.

Many places will take any of the cards. You've seen cash registers that are practically covered with various card system decals. But many department stores and specialty shops that don't accept bank cards will accept T&E cards.

If you carry an American Express card, you can use it to get money or traveler's checks from the American Express office during working hours, or from the American Express money machines which are located in major airports and other travel-related locations and operate 24 hours a day, 365 days a year. With the Gold Card you can cash a check for up to $1000 at an American Express office.

There is one substantive difference between bank cards and T&E cards when it comes to charging airline tickets. If you use a T&E card to charge your airline ticket, you are automatically covered by a fair amount of insurance in the event of accidental death or injury en route. The coverage varies slightly by company. The American Express coverage is for $75,000 and covers you on your way to the airport, in the terminals, in the plane, and on your way to your hotel or first stop. For $3.00 more, you can get $175,000 worth of additional coverage. Diner's Club is much the same except the $3.00 buys you $200,000 in additional insurance. Carte Blance has $60,000 automatic coverage with a $3.00 charge for an additional $150,000 in coverage.

Expense Accounts and Reimbursements

In a recent article in *Businesswoman*, the newsletter sponsored by Eastern Airlines, Editor Denise Berton point out that women consistently under report on their expense accounts. They do not claim all of the reimbursement to which they are honestly entitled. They subsidize the company's travel budget. They also tend to spend less than their male counterparts. Where a man will go out and spend $20.00 on dinner, a woman will only spend $7.00. A man will call to have his luggage picked up in his room and tip the bellhop a dollar while a woman will struggle down to the lobby by herself or pay the bellhop the "recommended minimum 50 cents per bag." A man might take a cab to the airport at $12.00 while the woman waits for the limo and saves the company $8.00. A man might be a big spender and take a client to dinner while the woman buys the customer a drink and then excuses herself to order a sandwich from room service.

In fairness, many of us do not care to eat and drink $20.00 worth of calories in the evening, and many men would look better and live longer if they opted for a lighter dinner as well. But on all of the other matters, female behavior is some combintion of our attitudes toward ourselves and our previous training. Unfortunately, many of the ways to save money on the road will interfere with your effectiveness. The objective of business and professional travel is to get the job done. It's not to accept the challenge to see the world on $5.00 a day. If you are saving money but causing undo wear and tear on your body or your mind, you and your employer will pay for it on the long run.

A great many women have not learned to value themselves and their time. "I'm not worth a $20 dinner," may be a way of seeking approval. "If I am a good little scout and conserve the company's resources, my boss will appreciate me more." Unfortunately, that backfires. Employers have certain expectations of on-the-road expenses. If your expense report is substantially below those expectations, it does two things. First, it makes the other people in the department look bad. You have become the equivalent of a rate buster. Some nitpicker somewhere will start to ask, "If she can spend three days in New York on $300, how come the rest of you are spending so much? The new per diem will be 20 percent less than last year." That would make you real popular.

If You Don't Think You're Worth It, Why Would Anyone Else?

Second, it says you don't think you're worth it, why would anyone else? Most people don't know what you're worth. They depend on you for cues. If you send off the message that you're not worth much more than a stay in a tent with peanut butter sandwiches, they're going to believe you.

Expense accounts are not incentives or perks. They are part of a system designed for reimbursing people for necessary business expenses. They are to be used to facilitate your professional activities. At a minimum, this means covering all of your out-of-pocket costs. and if you are significant to the company, your out-of-pocket expenses need not be chintzy. You need to be well taken care of if you are going to take care of the company's business. You need to be refreshed, rejuvenated, revitalized, and rewarded. Remember, you are representing your company. You need to feel good about yourself. That costs money. You do not need to sacrifice to prove your worthiness. You prove your worthiness by doing, not by doing without. If you don't value yourself, no one else will either.

You Prove Your Worthiness by Doing. Not By Doing Without

When you are on the road representing your employer, you have a responsibility to uphold your employer's image. If you take a client to a coffee shop for dinner, that isn't a reflection on you. It's a reflection on your employer. Rosalie got static from her boss after a convention because her expense account was so low. He wanted to know what she was doing when she should have been entertaining clients.

You need standards. Seek them out. Some accountants say that you aren't doing your best with your taxes unless you get challenged by the IRS. You may not want to be called on the carpet for excessive totals on your expense account, but you do want to stay within the respectable range. Find out what your auditors see as the normal expenditure patterns. Ask, "What is the normal amount budgeted per diem for travel?" It's okay to ask about money. It doesn't imply that you are trying to figure out a way to cheat your employer.

You may find that you are subject to some fairly stringent per diem limits. These can be a problem, since you can buy dinner in Arkansas for less than breakfast in New York. In Nevada they practically give the food away, expecting to get all the money back at the tables. You might as well find out in advance. It's a lot better to know what's expected of you. Check with the person who okays your expense reimbursement form before you leave to be sure that you collect the proper documentation. If your firm approves your expenses and reimburses you, you will have no problems with your personal tax situation.

If you will have unreimbursed business expenses, you must think about tax return requirements. Currently, the Internal Revenue Service requires receipts on any single expenditure of $25.00 or more. You can deduct expenditures of less than $25.00 without receipts, provided you keep a careful diary of your expenditures. Any office supply store has expense booklets designed for this purpose. But you must keep these records on a continuous basis. You can't keep them only when you are traveling.

When Money is Important

There is a great big difference between saving money and not wasting money. If you are traveling on your own nickel, or if money is important for other reasons, there are lots of options. Here are a few of the more significant ideas. Remember, the idea is to travel effectively. You are already putting out a lot of money for airfare, time off work, and hotels—even if you don't accomplish anything. To save $3.00 in cab fare and miss an important assignment is a case of the proverbial penny-wise and pound-foolish.

Of all of the meals, breakfast is the one where you get the least for your money. And besides, it's such a hassle and time waster. Carrying a zip lock bag of instant coffee, Tang, or a few tea bags and some Granola bars saves both time and money.

In lots of major downtown areas such as San Francisco, it's usually easier to hop on a bus for 50 cents than to hail a cab.

Either ask the driver if the bus is going as far as you need to go or be prepared to hop off if it takes a wrong turn.

You will save money simply by making sure that you only pay for those goods and services you receive. One of the sources of error is on your hotel bill. When you check out, the clerk will hand you the bill for verification of any charges against your room. There are always a lot of entries. There is the basic room rate, the tax, telephone, restaurant and room charges, and your dry cleaning bills. It's embarrassing to stand there counting on your fingers, so most people just pay up. If you find an error later, you usually let it go because it's such a pain to complain.

Paden Reeves has developed a system to cope with this problem. As Regional Manager for the Richard D. Irwin Company, he attends a lot of conventions and ends up charging a lot of things to his room. He even finds that people deliberately charge restaurant and cocktail lounge checks against his company suite without authorization. The hotel is supposed to verify all charges by checking that the person has a key to the room, but this step is often neglected. So Payden always selects a conference number. Say that his number is 7. Whenever he signs a check for rooms service, restaurant, cleaning, or any other tippable service, he always adds his tip in just the right amount so that the last digit of the bill comes out as a 7. If the check is $28.15, he tips $5.02. If its $3.10, he'll tip 47 cents. Then at checkout time he simply scans the very last column for any non-7 entries. If they are for room rate, tax, or telephone, they're acceptable. If a non-7 entry originated in the restaurant, he questions it. The hotel has to produce a copy of the receipt. If the signature doesn't match, it's the hotel's problem. His systems has saved him hundreds of dollars.

One of your best long run money savers is a complete listing of your expenses so that you can either claim them against your organization or your taxes. Think about the expenditures that slip through the cracks and develop a system to catch them.

Another good place to save money is on the telephone. The Bell System is made up of 17 different companies. Some of the policies and pricing structures vary as you move around the country. In New Orleans it is still a nickel to make a phone call from a phone booth. In Dallas, that will cost you a quarter. It pays to look at the local charges. Most hotels attach a surcharge to each call. It should be listed on a sticker on the telephone. That's worth it if you need the convenience or are making only a few calls. If you have a list of 10-20 calls, it may cost you $5.00 extra.

Time makes a tremendous difference in phone rates. If you are from the East and traveling West, you should plan to make calls back home and to your office before 8:00 AM. It saves you about 60 percent. If you are from the West and you go back East, waiting til after 5:00 PM will save you 35%, but if you can make the call to your family after 11:00 PM, you will still catch them up and you will be back to the 60 percent savings.

Ask your employer if you can get a credit card issued on the office phone number. If you make all of your hotel room long distance phone calls on a credit card number instead of a room number, you will be able to catch it if someone else deliberately or mistakenly charges long distance calls to your room. And while hotel bills simply list long distance charges, your telephone bill will give you a complete record of the number called, the time, and the charge. If your employer won't get you a credit card, have one issued on your home phone number. Again, the benefit is a complete record for expense account or tax purposes. Besides, you will never again have your call interrupted by the operator telling you, "Your three minutes are up. Please signal when finished." And you won't be standing there plunking 13 quarters into that slot. In many areas the telephone company is installing coinless phones for credit card holders. You don't even have to find that first dime.

Another way to save telephone money is to work *with* instead of working against the telephone operator system in the hotel. This is a tip to pass on to your co-workers, your spouse, or anyone else who might call you while you're on the road. When you call a hotel and ask for a person, the operator flips the key to ring that room, and turns to other in-coming and out-going calls. If you're not in, your caller can sit there listening to the phone ringing for an hour and the operator won't come back to take a message. The trick is to leave the message before letting the operator get away. Before asking the operator to ring your room, have your caller say, "I'd like to leave a message for Ms. You." The operator may take the message or divert the call to a message desk, but your caller is still dealing with a live human. After leaving the message, the caller can ask to be connected with your room. The message-taker may sigh in disgust, but your call will be transferred back to the operator who will then ring your room. If the call gets through, the message-leaver tells you that there's a message but you can ignore it. If the call doesn't get through, the person doesn't have to hang on the line hoping to get back to the operator.

There are lots of ways to use money efficiently. Remember, in all of your money matters a little planning and a self-respecting attitude can help you to do the best job of achieving your professional objectives with the least wear and tear on your physical and emotional self.

Chapter 8
Relaxation and Mental Health

It is a happy talent to know how to play.
—Ralph Waldo Emerson

After the Christmas and New Year's holidays, most people are happy to get back to work where they can get some rest. Travel is like Christmas, New Year's Eve, and the Fourth of July wrapped into one. It can bring on more stress and anxiety than any of these events. And it builds geometrically. The stress is worth it, but it's still stress. Unless you get yourself together with some routine to relieve the stress and tension, you'll end up a nervous wreck.

The physical and emotional demands of travel can bring on counterproductive reactions, or they can be managed in ways that make us even more productive. Tension relieving strategies are just as important to effective travel as packing or any of the other more tangible activities.

A proper attitude is a good starting point. Experienced travelers will urge you to be good to yourself. With all its virtues, travel still delivers continuing assaults on both your physical and mental being. It is no time to sacrifice or to endure. A little pampering is essential. How can you be good to yourself? You can take the time and make an extra effort to meet both your physical and your emotional needs. Too many people view their travel time as a sort of time warp or period of suspended animation. It's part of your life, too.

Too Many People View Their Travel Time as a Sort of Time Warp or Period of Suspended Animation. It's Part of Your Life, Too.

Guilt plays a big part in this problem. We can justify being away from our family, our friends, and our plants as long as we are *working*. But to relax and enjoy ourselves in the process seems hedonistic. If your employer is paying the bills, it seems that you should be struggling to be productive, not out having a good time. But how many hours a day can you be productive? If you've put in a normal work day, you deserve some relaxation. Physical activities provide one solution.

Physical Fitness

Even if you maintain a regular exercise program at home, it's easy to let it slide while you're traveling. There are so many obstacles. It's tough sticking to your normal schedule. At home you may run in the morning, but if you have to catch a plane or be on the road to the next stop, running loses out. Things are out of sync. You may have free time, but at all the wrong times. Who wants to run alone in a strange place after dark? And you miss your normal facilities. Say you belong to a tennis club at home. When you want to play, you have a listing of potential partners and you are somewhat aware of their skill levels and availability. It's a lot more difficult to find a suitable tennis partner in a strange city.

In-Room Exercising You may be reluctant to venture out to find facilities or partners. If so, you can still absolve some of your guilt by exercising in your room. And you can even do it stark naked. One of these days the hotels with the in-house TV movie channels might be nice enough to run one channel with the Jack LaLanne type exercise shows so we won't have to exercise alone. But until then, you'll have to build your own routine.

About the easiest exercise equipment to take on the road is jumprope. Supposedly 15 minutes of rope jumping is worth a mile of running. The person in the room below you won't mind too much as long as you do it before the end of the 11:00 PM news. Hotel rooms are also great places for stretching exercises. If you flip the blanket and sheet off the end of the bed leaving it tucked in on the bottom you have a clean padded surface for your exercises. You can do your routine of sit-ups, toe touches, and leg lifts while you watch TV.

Running and Other Sports Even if you don't exercise regularly at home, don't neglect this part of your life while you're on the road. Exercise is a great way to relieve stress. If you are a runner, go ahead and pack your shoes. People all over the country are running in all kinds of weather. Some hotels such as the Rye Town Hilton in Rye, New York, and the Hyatt Regency in San Francisco even offer Par courses that include a running trail and a variety of exercise stops. If tennis is your game, you'll find that lots of folks travel with their racquets. Some organizations, such as the racquet club associations, even have reciprocal clubhouse arrangements. Inquire at your home club. You can find out more about the facilities for your favorite sports by reading specialized magazines. There are even entire books devoted to the subject, such as *Tennis for Travelers* by Gilbert Richards. Many hotels have standing arrangements with nearby health facilities. If your favorite sport requires special conditions or facilities, ask when you make your hotel reservation. On my first trip to Austin, Texas, I took my roller skates. WRONG. While I tend to see Texas as flat, based on my trips to Dallas and Houston, Austin is in the hill country.

Most hotels have heated pools and whirlpools. These are great tension relievers. The problem is getting to them. Too many of them are either isolated on a scarey floor or featured in a glassed off section to the lobby so you become a floor show for the other guests. That takes a strong ego. Some of the newer luxury hotels have both sports elevators and back doors so that you don't have to sneak through the lobby in your sweaty duds.

Regardless of where you go, you can always walk. Walking is one of the best exercises of all. One beautiful October Saturday in New York City, I walked from my hotel at 55th Street and Fifth Avenue all the way down to 34th Street, over to Seventh Avenue, back up to Central Park, over to Bloomingdale's at 63rd and Third Avenue, and back to my hotel. That's about 60 blocks. It took most of the day and I felt great. By the way, roller skates are okay in Manhattan. A man skated past me on Seventh Avenue and on the weekends they rent skates in Central Park.

Roller Skates Are Okay in Manhattan.

You should walk briskly from the hotel until you start to feel a bit tired and then walk back. In the hotels that are attached to a mall, you can go for a long walk through the mall without worrying about the weather or safety. Strolling doesn't count. If you have enough time, you can also skip cabs and walk to appointments. Before you walk off into strange territory, however, ask the bell captain if it is safe.

In-Flight Exercises If you are traveling a long way on the plane, you should be doing some exercises in flight. Both SAS and Lufthansa Airlines publish booklets of inobtrusive in-flight exercises. For example, one is to loosen your seatbelt and lean forward as if to retrieve something from your carry-on baggage. A second is to stretch your head back as if to look over the seat in back of you. You can cross your legs and do ankle circles. You can stretch your right arm up to reach up for the airvent and then stretch your left arm up for the light. You can also tighten the muscles in your buttocks, hold for a count of 30, and relax. A series of these at least makes you feel like you're doing something. The objective is not so much fitness as the improvement of your circulation. Unless you give your blood vessels a little help in their efforts to shoot your blood back to your heart to be reoxygenated, gravity drags it all down into your feet and legs. The results are both swollen feet and light-headedness. At least get up and walk down the aisle a few times. If you feel you need an excuse, walk up and get magazines out of the rack. This is just one of the points in favor of an aisle seat. And by the way, most of these in-flight exercises are also very helpful in long meetings.

Personal Care Routines

Looking good is a big step toward feeling good. Taking care of yourself while you are traveling means attending to your normal personal care routines. A droopy hair-do or chipped nail polish is depressing. But you have to be careful to schedule the time for these things. You can't do a manicure or a touch-up on your hair coloring during the afternoon coffee break. That takes more planning than nontravelers would imagine. Most travelers never even get to watch the evening news or read the newspaper.

Lynn Redgrave, co-host of NBC's "Not For Women Only," recommends that you have your hairdresser take pictures of your hair when it is in its best condition. Then when you go into a strange salon with hair that doesn't look like you want it to look, you can easily communicate the desired outcome.

When I travel by car, I use my driving time as drying time for my nail polish. One day I was standing beside my car painting my nails on the roof while the amused attendant filled my tank and checked my oil. I was proud of myself for having shown the foresight to extract my credit card from my card case before starting to paint. He carefully handed me the pen to sign the charge form and even opened the door for me to get in. It was only after he had closed the door and moved on to another customer that I realized I had, through force of habit, pocketed my car key. Have you ever tried to get a car key out of a skirt pocket while seated in a small car without ruining your new coat of nail polish?

Look upon your time on the road as an opportunity to do some of those things you don't want to do in the presence of the other people in our life. Doris Day revealed one of her beauty secrets: Once a month she coats herself in Vaseline, climbs into her flannel pajamas, and hops in bed for the night. Now that is strictly a solitary activity. You may want to pack your flannel pajamas, but what about two pairs of white socks. Slather Vaseline on your hands and feet and slip on the socks. In the morning you will have much smoother skin.

Leisure Time

A dreaded occurence is to be caught away from home over the weekend. Some people can handle travel as long as they are busy, but give them some free time and they turn into basket cases. A pleasant hotel room can turn into a prison cell in about 11 hours no matter how gripping the novel. What are you to do? First, a tip from Al Borcover of the Chicago Tribune:

> Always plan your day off. Get a city magazine, stop at the desk, ask the flight attendant, but get some idea and plan your day. Otherwise you will be slow to get up, slow to get started, and end up talking yourself out of any worthwhile activity. As the day goes on you will get even more depressed. Plan your time off just as carefully as you plan your work day.

See the Sights   There are lots of things you can do. Some travelers never see anything but the inside of a hotel, a saloon, a restaurant, a cab, an airport, and an airplane. These all look pretty much the same. Only the accents differ. There are so many other things to do on the road. One is to play tourist. Everyplace, no matter how maligned, has its points of interest. Anyone who hides in a hotel room in New York, San Francisco, Los Angeles, New Orleans, Chicago, San Diego, Boston, Washington, Atlanta, Minneapolis, or one of our other great cities is beyond hope. To do so is either downright lazy or incredibly cowardly.

But even the cities that get less favorable press—the Detroits, Clevelands, Baltimores, Pittsburghs, Buffalos, Fargos, and the Fresnos of the world—have something to offer, if *you* make the effort. No one is going to knock on your door and hand you a great day. If you don't want to go it alone, there is nothing wrong with taking the local bus tour. You'll find it listed in the Yellow Pages or you can check with the hotel. If you go back to the same city regularly, you may want to ask the telephone company for a copy of that telephone book. It makes it easier for both business and pleasure purposes. Another trick is to subscribe to the local newspaper—at least the Sunday edition. Playing tourist can be great fun—even if you do it all alone.

Think of the benefits of being a solitary tourist. You can do exactly what you want. You don't have to please anyone else. If you want to linger in one spot and skip another entirely, it's up to you. If your feet are tired, you can sit down without holding someone else up. I once rented a car and drove out along the route of the Revolutionary War battle between Boston and Concord. The facilities there had been well developed to accommodate the crowds during the Bicentennial. There is a little national park service facility with displays depicting the important historical events. Mine was the only car in the huge lot. The park officer on duty was thrilled to see me. She asked if I wanted to see the five-minute movie and set it up just for me. When that was finished she escorted me into a 50 seat theater to view the 20-minute film. I'm sure I made her day. I couldn't help but think that a few years before tourists must have been lined up out into the street for a chance to crowd in on the park service's schedule to see the same films I had viewed in comfort at my convenience.

> Some People Go Through Life Willing to Give Almost Anything a Fling if There Is the Outside Chance That It Will Be Fun.

There are so many people who talk themselves out of things before they even try them. They miss so much. Some people go through life willing to give almost anything a fling if there is the outside chance that it will be fun. Others aren't willing to try anything without a guarantee that it is going to be a roaring success. Who do you think gets the most out of life?

Nancy is a financial planner for a major corporation. You might describe her as a serious conservative. She made a business trip to Los Angeles. it was her first trip to that city. Her local contact suggested that she should see Disneyland. Nancy attempted to conceal her dismay. But the contact persisted. Nancy capitulated. She's big enough to admit that she was wrong. While she did forego "Mr. Toad's Wild Ride," she was honestly impressed with the flowers, the quality of the attractions, the musical groups performing in the restaurants and courtyards, and especially with the Bell Telephone Company's free presentation, "America the Beautiful." She admits that she would have avoided this "frivolity," had it not been for the persistance of her local contact and that it would have been her loss.

I hadn't been horseback riding since a childhood vacation to the Grand Tetons. I was at a conference at a full service resort that offered guided horseback riding. One of the other women wanted to go. I wasn't quite prepared, but donned my white slacks, yellow T-shirt, and Famolare sandals to give it a try. My behind still hurts when I think about it. So I didn't like it. How would I have known if I hadn't tried it? Bernice had a great time!

Pursue Your Special Interests Some of the happiest travelers are those who develop an area of interest and pursue it in each city they visit. It may be architecture, art museums, libraries, history, zoos, universities, retail stores, manufacturing plant tours, local theaters, antiques, bridges, coin collections, geneology, or any other hobby area. The point is that they have some interest that inspires them to get out to see things or meet people. They view their travel as an opportunity to expand on their knowledge of their chosen interest. Roz Barrie is an attorney. She travels to take depositions and meet with clients in other cities. She is developing a network of bridge-playing associates. She lets them know when she is coming and makes her own opportunities to unwind over the card table.

Even if you don't have a strong interest in a hobby, you owe it to yourself to sample the special interest of the area. If you are in Seattle, you might take a walk along the waterfront. You don't like fishing? Have you ever tried it in Seattle? If you are in Kentucky, you should try the horse races. In New Orleans it's jazz. Every location has something to offer. If you show some flexibility, you can really enjoy yourself. Your travel agent has all the information, if you ask. Borcover recommends starting a travel file. If you see something interesting in the paper or on television, file it away according to the state or the city. Then you'll have someplace to start.

You might just choose to do something you don't take the time to do at home. One veteran traveler always treats himself to a movie. Now, that's not too exotic, but he doesn't take the time to go to movies when he's at home.

Shop for a Change   If you are like most professional women, you hardly have time to stroll around in stores enjoying the view. Most professional women dash in, grab what they need, and dash out. You might use some of your free time to shop. Who knows? It may even turn into an event. Jerry was in Dallas and figured he just had to stop in at the famous Neiman Marcus Department Store. He just wanted to see what it's like and thought he might send a gift to his wife. As he wandered around, he noticed workers setting up a bar. He asked why and found out that there was to be a cocktail reception for a famous artist who supplied them with very expensive registered porcelain bird figurines. He expressed some interest and managed to get himself invited. On the spot, the clerk addressed an engraved invitation. He went back to his hotel, cleaned up, and returned to rub shoulders with some of Dallas' finest citizens. He had a great evening.

If you go shopping, you can run into two problems. The first is that you now have more to pack. Here's a tip: Have the merchandise sent to your home. If you are in a different state, merchandise sent to your home is not subject to local sales tax. Even if you have to pay the postage, you have saved perhaps 4-6 percent on the purchase price and you don't have to carry it. I bought two suits in Chicago. The store charged me a $5.00 mailing fee on each suit, but the sales tax would have been about $10.00 per suit. I saved money and the suits beat me home.

The second problem is paying for the things you buy. Many of the more prestigious department and specialty stores do not accept Visa and MasterCard. Some of these will accept American Express or another T&E card. Stores like Lord and Taylor's, Marshall Field's, Bloomingdale's, Tiffany's, and Sak's Fifth Avenue are examples. If you don't have enough cash or an acceptable card, don't despair. Any store worth it's salt will open a charge account for you at the register station if you will simply fill out the application. Before you open an account, check to see if they will accept any of your other department store charge cards. Most department stores are affiliated with groups such as the Carter Hawley Hale group that includes Weinstocks, Capwells, The Emporium, The Broadway, Neiman Marcus, and Bergdorf Goodman. Some of the stores in a group will have reciprocal credit system. You could use you Weinstock's card at The Emporium.

> **Any Store Worth Its Salt Will Open a Charge Account for You at the Register Station if You Will Simply Fill Out the Application.**

These new accounts are often limited to $50.00. If you want to spend more, visit the credit office. If you can supply other charge cards and the name of your bank, they will extend additional credit. The processing might take an hour, but you can do your shopping during that time. Perhaps you'll never need the card again. There's no great loss.

The Obligation Trap It's one thing to go shopping for your own pleasure and benefit. It's another to end up running errands. One of the traps to avoid is the "Obligation Trap." Don't let people burden you with what you should do while you are in town. It's your time and your energy. Say you grew up in Detroit and were going back there to a business meeting. If you don't want to visit your aunts and cousins, or look up a friend of a friend, don't do it. Don't feel guilty. Don't make apologies. Don't even let them know you're in town if you don't want to.

Don't promise to do favors for others unless it brings you satisfaction. Jane's sister-in-law collects Jim Beam bottles. They come in all kinds, which are listed in a catalog and are far more valuable than the bourbon inside. In fact, the sister-in-law is a teetotaler and pours the bourbon down the drain. Some of these bottles are produced for particular events such as a city's centennial celebration and are hard to get since the liquor can't be shipped across state lines. When Jane went to Chicago, her sister-in-law asked her to go to the suburb of Lombard just to buy a Beam bottle shaped like a lilac bush. Jane did it, but she learned her lesson. It didn't look that far on the map but it was a $30.00

round-trip in a cab from the loop and took over an hour. It didn't make her very happy. If someone asks you to pick up something while you are in New York, just answer, "I'm not sure that I'll have time."

Even though you are on a business trip, you can't be all business. You need some time to yourself to attend to both your physical and emotional needs. You need some enjoyment and personal satisfaction. You not only need it, you deserve it.

Chapter 9
Conferences and Other Special Destinations

"One percent of the people do everything, another 2 percent stand around watching, and 97 percent aren't really sure what happened."
—Ben Franklin

There are some very special destinations—times and places where you step out of your everyday professional routine for some specific and worthwhile purpose. Conferences, professional meetings, seminars, special training schools conducted by your employer or your suppliers, and sales meetings are the most common events. Some people look upon these events as ordeals and use them as another chance to practice their avoidance techniques. They either look for excuses to skip the event entirely or they drag themselves to it and participate grudgingly or, even worse, create negative waves and disparage the honest efforts of others.

Other people will go anywhere at any time as long as someone else is paying the bills. As far as they can see, these events are vacations. They could care less about the objectives of the conference planners or the intentions of their employers in sending them to the meetings. They are there to have a good time. They see these events as an excuse to misbehave.

The real winners are the people who carefully evaluate these extra-curricular opportunities, select those events that could be meaningful, and then develop strategies and practices to get the most out of the experience. The people who make things happen are serious about participating in activities germane to their professions. While others are just standing in the bleachers watching the game go on, the participators are in the game. Sure, they have a little fun while they're at it, but they participate with a purpose.

Why Are Conferences Important?

Going to a conference says two things about you. First, it says you are willing to invest your own time in your own professional development. While other people are spending the weekend working on their tans or having their locks frosted, you are working on your head. You are willing to disrupt your normal schedule, go to the expense and inconvenience of being away from home, and assume the risks that go along with this in expectation of self-improvement.

Beyond that, attending conferences says that someone else is willing to invest dollars in your investment in your head. That's no joke. Attending a conference costs lots of money and takes you away from your normal duties. Someone has to pay for your expenses and your time. It may be your employer. Later in this chapter we will go into the techniques that you can use to get your boss to provide increased support for your professional travel. You may be paying the bill yourself. That's not all bad. Regina is now a well known authority in her field. She traces her good fortune to the determination she felt when she started attending professional conferences on her own nickel.

Virginia Lofft, Editor of *Successful Meetings*, has seen a lot of conferences and what they can do for people. Here is her advice:

> By all means, grab every opportunity that becomes available to attend meetings as a participant or as someone on the program. Being there gives you an opportunity to learn the latest developments in your particular field and gives you prestigious visibility in your own industry. Good note-taking during conferences also gives you an opportunity when you return to your office to share new ideas, trends, etc., with other executives in your organization.
>
> Try to get on the program whenever possible. One of the best ways to ease into this role is to volunteer to be a panelist when a subject you know something about is being covered.

This is the best way to gain valuable public exposure and recognition. By all means, develop moderator skills and leadership skills as early in your career as possible. These skills are important and result in frequent invitations to participate in conferences and conventions. These invitations add to the luster of your reputation in your own organization.

One of the exciting things about a conference is that you get to see the really big names in your field. Every field has its big names. In women's rights it's Steinem and Friedan. In data processing it's Captain Grace Murray Hopper and Dr. Ruth Davis. In economics it's Samuelson and Friedman. You get to find out that these people are human, only human. They are not, regardless of everything you have seen in magazines and on TV—repeat, they are *not* seven feet tall! Light does not radiate from their foreheads. They are real live honest-to-goodness human beings just like the rest of us. They may look better or worse than their pictures. They may be pleasant or unpleasant. They may say clever, provocative things or just stand there.

Over ten years ago I attended a convention sponsored by one of the major professional organizations in my field, the American Marketing Association. About five years prior to that, as a beginning marketing student, I had used the leading text in the field. There, in living reality, stood E. Jerome McCarthy, Ph.D., the author of the textbook. It was almost more than I could stand. I just stood there gawking. He didn't look that unusual, but his name tag almost flashed. The man was engaged in conversation. As the people drifted away he became aware of me. He looked up and politely asked, "Can I help you?" Cleverly I mumbled, "I just wanted to look at you."

Well, the story goes on. Later in my career—at least two years later—I was teaching at a midwestern university. Another member of the faculty was working on his doctorate and one of his professors was our author friend. I confided, "I met him at the national meeting," and went on to tell my tale. My colleague later came back and reported that he had mentioned the incident to McCarthy and that he not only remembered it well, but had been quite pleased with my comment.

Attending conferences allows you to keep up with new developments in your field. One of the fastest changing fields in the world, and incidently one in which women are assuming increasing responsibilities, is electronic information processing. Edward Palmer, Executive Director of the 30,000 member strong Data

Processing Management Association, recognizes the value of conferences and seminars when he says,

> Because the rate of knowledge obsolescence in the information processing industry is so rapid, you can easily become an endangered species by standing still. It really amounts to a question of survival, which can be achieved only by an intensive self-improvement effort involving attendance at meetings, conferences, and seminars which will enhance your professional skills.

How Do You Find Out About Conferences?

There are lots of conferences. Most are sponsored by professional organizations. There are also thousands of seminars that are sponsored by organizations or by private seminar companies. These sponsors send announcements to business firms, government agencies, educational institutions, and individuals. If you aren't getting the notices, someone else in your organization is getting them and isn't posting them or passing them around. It is really simple to stop by the mail room and ask the clerk where these notices are being directed. One of the frequent repositories is the personnel office.

One of the better places to find out about professional conferences is in professional newspapers or journals in your field. Almost all of them have a "conference calendar" feature. You can also check the public library for a copy of "World Convention Dates." Published by the Hendrickson Publishing Company in Hempstead, New York, it lists tons of up-coming conventions by city and gives you the name of the person to contact for more information.

You will get direct mail notices if your name is on mailing lists because of your magazine subscriptions, your charge cards, or any other activities associated with professionals. Don't be upset when your "junk mail" clutters your desk. Recognize it as a status symbol. The higher your socio-economic status, the more you get.

Another important channel of information is through professional organizations. Even if you never attend a single conference, you should seriously consider membership in the major organization in your field. Your employer may pay your membership or the costs of attending local luncheon or dinner meetings. Of course, you have to ask for the support. What have you got to lose?

The worst thing that can happen is that your boss will say no. And just by asking you have made one more statement about your professionalism and career orientation. Even if your employer won't pay, these professional expenses are tax deductible.

The Worst Thing That Can Happen Is That Your Boss Will Say No.

There is an organization for everybody. If you don't know the choices in your field, ask around your office and see who belongs to what. If you don't get enough answers, go to the library and ask to see a copy of the *Encyclopedia of Associations*. It gives you all associations listed by key words. Some associations focus on a specific industry, such as data processing. You can check Accounting, Education, Real Estate, Medicine, Law, Sales, Government, or any other field. Other associations, such as the National Association for Professional Saleswomen, cross industry lines and focus on a particular type of occupation. The Encyclopedia gives you the size of the organization, its address, and other important facts that will help you decide if it is the one for you.

Sometimes the local chapter is less than exciting. It takes a lot of work to run a good chapter. Too many people limit their horizon to the local chapter and write off the value of membership in the national organization. Think of it this way: If the local chapter is weak, there will be more opportunities for you to make a contribution and a name for yourself among the professionals in your community.

Even if there isn't a local chapter, you can usually join the national organization. When you travel, you can take advantage of your membership to meet other professionals in your field. Most chapters of professional organizations are quite pleased to have an out-of-town visitor at their dinner meeting. You will be treated as a celebrity. Some organizations, such as Sales and Marketing Executives, publish an annual directory that lists chapters nationwide and gives information on the normal meeting night, the officers, and the size of the chapter. Armed with your membership card and national directory, you have instant friends in almost any city.

Jo Foxworth, author of *Boss Lady,* strongly recommends active membership in business societies. Like anything else, the opportunities are there for those who have the foresight and courage to grasp them. She says:

> Associations give you a showcase for your talents, a platform for your ideas and opinions, a chance to grow in new directions meaningful in your career.
>
> 1. Get your company's full blessing at the start. If Mr. Omnipotence doesn't know what the organization does, fill him in—with emphasis on the professional activities.
> 2. Volunteer for visible projects that will showcase your talents to the business community.
> 3. Get involved in work you haven't been doing. Grow in new directions.
> 4. Surround yourself with enthusiastic, conscientious members who can be relied on to do not only their own jobs, but those of the sudden flameouts.
> 5. Make all the friends you can. These contacts can be enormously valuable in getting needed information in a hurry—or in getting another job.

Some organizations specialize in conducting educational seminars. The American Management Association is an example. AMA offers thousands of seminars each year on all kinds of management subjects. You can obtain their catalog by writing them at 135 West 50th Street, New York, NY 10020.

Seminars are often sponsored by universities. This is usually through the School of Business or the Office of Continuing Education. You can obtain information on their programs by contacting your local university.

How Do I Get To Go?

Imagine this: Your boss hustles into your office waving a registration form for the national conference and yelling, "You've just got to go to this. It will be great. Don't worry, I'll cover all the costs." Do you find that hard to imagine? It doesn't happen very often and, if it does, it's usually because you are going to be expected to spend 18 hours a day on your feet in the company booth in the exhibit area passing out sales literature and writing orders. If you want to register as a participant at a conference or seminar, you are going to have to sell your boss on the idea.

Your Mission Is to Help Your Boss See Why It Is in Everyone's Best Interest That You Get to Go to the Conference.

Before you begin your selling effort, make sure that you have something to sell. Spend some time evaluating the alternatives and pick the seminar or conference that seems to make the most sense—that has the most to offer. If it's your first try, don't waste it on a pseudo-professional cruise/seminar to Nassau. Either pick a seminar directly related to your most important work responsibilities or a conference sponsored by a credible professional organization. Make it easy for yourself. Learn as much as you can about the conference. Read the brochure carefully and call or write for more information if you have questions. You are going to need all the information as you proceed in your campaign. And it is a campaign. You have an objective in mind. Remember, your mission is to help your boss see why it is in everyone's best interest that you get to go to the conference.

Dr. Dorri Jacobs, author of the book *Priorities,* offers these tips for evaluating educational workshops:

1. Know why you are going and what you hope to accomplish.
2. Read the descriptions carefully: Look for specific course goals.
3. Comparison shop. Check against similar workshops as to program content, scope, method, length, price.
4. Scan the teachers' or presenters' bios for experience, training, credentials, background, approach.
5. Research the legitimacy and the track record of the organization sponsoring the workshop you're considering. Can you talk to anyone who's already attending one?
6. Ask questions! You have a right to know: the maximum enrollment, level of participants, workshop aims and techniques, and any additional "special charges."

Selling isn't all that difficult. It's just a matter of helping someone else see why he or she is better off to give you what you want. You want to go to the conference. What does your boss want? How are you going to harmonize these objectives? Just put yourself in your boss's shoes. Ask yourself, "Why would I want to send someone who worked for me to a conference?" It certainly isn't so that her desk chair will get a vacation.

Setting the Stage The key to successful selling is preparation. A good saleswoman does her research and then takes that information and develops a sales plan. This plan involves four elements. First is the approach: How are you going to bring up the subject and gain your employer's interest? Second is your presentation, the period when you make your points in favor of attending the conference. Third is the close. This is the hardest part for most people. It is the part when you ask your boss for a commitment. You ask for action. And finally there is follow-up. You have to make sure that your boss continues to feel comfortable with the decision and doesn't cancel on you at the last minute.

In planning your approach, use time to your advantage. Notices on these conferences are available up to a year in advance. You can usually run up waving a check and register at the door, but it's a good idea to give yourself at least a month just to make plans for travel, at home, and at work. Besides, if you have done your homework and found a really worthwhile event, it may be sold out. Lots of people will be going.

The National Computer Conference is an annual event sponsored by the American Federation of Information Processing Societies, a consortium of 13 information processing associations. It draws about 80,000 people. Most cities don't have that many houses let alone hotel rooms. It's so large that they can only hold it in a few places like New York City, Chicago, and Anaheim. If you don't make your plans early, you can end up sleeping on the curb.

It's smart to begin to build some groundwork for your proposal long before you make it. Start to feed your boss some information on the organization or the problem. "Say, have you seen what they are doing through the National Association of Credit Managers?" or "We sure are having problems with our customer service levels. I wish I could find some materials that would help me develop a better system for handling that." Don't ask your boss for any advice or commitment. Just start to mention things and focus attention on the area in which you have the interest.

Wait for the Moment When You Are Basking in Accomplishment—When Your Halo Is on Straight.

Don't be impatient. Pick the right time to bring up the conference. That's not Friday afternoon or Monday morning. Wait for the moment when you are basking in accomplishment—when your halo is on straight. You are going to have to sell your boss on the idea. Remember, your boss isn't asking you to go, so your boss isn't interested in working too hard to figure out why you should go. And just wanting to go isn't enough.

Grace had made several attempts and was never able to get her boss to sit down and talk about any of the programs she suggested. He always had excuses. She finally decided that his real problem was that he didn't know enough about the kind of seminars she was suggesting and was afraid that he would be put on the spot. She had a great idea. She got to work and prepared an extensive report on the topic of conferences. It categorized seminars and seminar sponsors. It included guidelines for evaluating seminars and lots of other information on locations, schedules, and prices. It was a lot of work.

One day she walked into his office and casually said, "Here is that seminar report you asked me to do." Her boss was somewhat puzzled. He didn't remember giving that assignment, but no one does anything without orders. Grace didn't press him. She waited a week or so and then went back in to say, "Say, if you've had the chance to look at that report, could we set up a time to talk about it?" Now, notice she didn't press him for any proof that he had read the report. If she had said, "What did you think about my report?" she would have been putting him on the spot again. He might have come out with a negative, "It just isn't in our best interest at this time." There was a real fine chance that he hadn't read the report yet. But how could he acknowledge that? He had to set up the appointment. And then he had to read the report to get ready. She had him under her control. Once she cleared the approach hurdle, the rest of the sale was easy. She got clearance for her seminars.

Delivering Your Message Once you have your employer's attention, you'd better have something to say. And it pays to say it from your listener's viewpoint. You need to make points that center around the reasons why this activity will improve your performance and productivity. Either one of those is going to make your boss look good. Remember, most people act in their own best interests as they see them.

It may be that you are going to learn important new skills.

This is a particularly good line of reasoning if you are in a technologically advancing area such as medicine or data processing. To emphasize this point, make sure to read the program carefully and pick out two or three sessions that will appeal to your boss. Tell why you need to work on these skills and why this conference or seminar is the best way to do that. It is your responsibility to convince your boss that the organizations holding the program is legitimate.

Most People Act in Their Own Best Interests as They See Them.

Glenys Zimrick is an accountant. She learned of a special course offered through a university over 2000 miles away. She checked it out thoroughly and then sold the partners in her firm on the idea of sending her to attend the two-week long session. Her basic selling point was that the course would give her the knowledge she needed to better serve the firm's clients in the area of estate planning. She helped the partners to view her travel expenses as an investment that would pay off in increased profitability.

If you are responsible for purchasing any kinds of equipment or supplies, pay careful attention to any vender exhibits being held in conjunction with the convention. You can point out that the conferene will give you the opportunity to talk with all of the venders in the exhibit area. This means that you may learn about some products or services that could improve productivity or reduce costs. Besides, you can do this all at one time instead of having to spend hours listening to individual sales presentations.

This book was written on a Wang Word Processor—a $12,000 computerized typewriter system. I didn't know a single thing about word processors until I visited the exhibits at a Data Processing Management Association conference in Anchorage, Alaska, in June, 1978. Just learning about this machine was enough to make the trip worthwhile. This book has taken me about half as long and has caused less than one-third the aggravation of my first book, *Saleswoman,* which was pecked out on a portable electric.

You may want to alert your boss to the ways you can spread the benefits of the conference to other people in your organization. "I'd really be happy to take the responsibility of preparing a report on the sessions I attend and sharing that information with the other people in my department. I know Jennifer has been interested in this subject." Perhaps you could offer to bring back your evaluations of various sessions. "I know we will be planning our sales meeting soon and I'll be happy to tell you if any of the speakers at the convention seem to fit any of the slots at our fall meeting."

To get support, you must phrase your comments in terms of the best interests of your boss and your organization. You must be able to show enthusiasm and to show confidence in the organization sponsoring the program. If you go in to your boss and say, "I don't know if it's worth my time to go to this, but I thought I'd check with you before I threw out the announcement," you can go home and throw out your suitcase, too. People do that because they lack confidence in their worth or their own judgment. They want someone else to take the responsibility for making the decision. Then if things don't turn out as well as they would like, they can always lean on, "Well, it wasn't my idea to go to that dumb conference." Don't expect your boss to talk you into going.

Don't Expect Your Boss to Talk You Into Going.

Be prepared to offer an estimate of the expenses. Don't be skimpy. Be sure to figure airfare, ground transportation, hotels, meals, tips, and registration fees. State your estimate with confidence. Don't cringe or apologize. Remember, you're worth it. A very important point to remember is that your boss will probably have to defend your absence and the expenses to someone else higher up or to your co-workers who are left in the office while you're off "running around and having a good time." Your job is to make that an easy task. If you give your boss all of the ammunition to go to the next in command and made a credible presentation, you will improve your chances considerably. If you come back with some worthwhile knowledge or other evidence that you were serious about the conference, you may well get to go again.

Expect your boss to raise some objections. It's just unbosslike not to. Try to figure out what they will be. "We just have too much work here. We can't get along without you," or "If I send you, everybody else will want to go and we just can't afford that." Another good one is the delaying comment, "There are always lots of conferences. Let's skip this one and catch one later on." Make a list of possible objections beforehand and plan your response. If you're not prepared, you'll cave in at the first objection. If you have your responses ready it gives you a big ego boost. Don't give up easily. And don't wait for your boss to say, "Fine, that looks like a great idea. Do it."

Ask For a Commitment More selling efforts fail for lack of a closing than for any other single reason. The close is the point where you ask your boss for a commitment. Good closes make it easier for the person to do it the way you want than to do anything else. They are stated in the positive form almost assuming that the answer will be YES. "So we agree that this looks good. Fine, I'll make my reservations and take care of the details here in the office." This comment is a lot better than, "Well, do you mind if I plan to go?" One of the really good techniques is to give your boss a choice between two alternatives which are equally desirable to you. "Would you prefer that I leave on Sunday and get back on Wednesday or leave on Monday and get back on Thursday?" Even if you boss opts for Monday to Wednesday, you're way ahead of a flat NO.

Use the ploy that so many kids use on their parents. The kid asks his mother if he can stay up all night and while she's reeling he sneaks by with his consolation request, which is to stay up til 11:00 to watch the end of a monster movie. That's all he wanted in the first place. Ask to go to the national conference in New York City and then watch your boss's look of relief when you offer to settle for the regional meetings in Kansas City.

Should You Be Willing to Pay? Some organizations are well off and accustomed to giving out free rides. That's real nice. But if you are among the millions who work for fiscally conservative organizations, you may find that your boss is going to suggest that you make some effort to reduce expenses. You may be encouraged to share a room and to take the red eye flights. You may be given a per diem expense limitation. With the cost of hotel rooms and meals in many convention cities, this per diem may not cover your actual out-of-pocket expenses. Does that mean that you shouldn't go? What if your boss will give you the time off, but won't pay any of the bills. Limiting reimbursements is one way of saying NO without saying NO. Most people decide that it wasn't so important to go anyway. Should you stay home?

Paying all or part of the expenses to go to a conference has its own advantages. For one thing, it really motivates you to get something out of the experience. Second, it clearly demonstrates to everyone that you have a serious commitment to your professional advancement. All of those sour-grapers who downgrade conferences as boondogles have to take notice. It separates you from the cry-babies and short-run optimizers who can't see out of their own little ruts. And it really eliminates any guilt you might have felt if you just happen to encounter someone who offers you a better job. Some people are afraid to pick up part or all of the expenses one time for fear of establishing a precedent. It all depends on how you handle it. You can use it as a bargaining point for the next event. "Remember, last year I paid a share of my expenses. I think that shows that I'm really sincerely interested and think that on that basis, it would be worth your full support this year."

All of Those Sour-Grapers Who Downgrade Conferences as Boondogles Have to Take Notice.

Follow-Up Once you have your clearance, you still have some follow-up work to do. Make sure that you get all of the paperwork and travel planning done as soon as possible. Feed your boss an occasional tidbit on the value of the experience. "I got a copy of the final schedule and it really looks good." Make sure that you have your work covered. And take some actions to ensure a successful experience.

Preconference Preparation

There is more to getting ready for a conference than packing, making reservations, and taking your dog to the kennel. You have to prepare yourself mentally and plan your strategy. Ask yourself what you expect to get out of the conference. There are a lot of legitimate answers:

- To increase my visibility
- To learn more about my profession
- To meet influential people
- To meet other people just like me
- To keep track of the job market
- To see new products
- To test my people skills
- To increase my enthusiasm for my profession

- To widen my horizons
- All of the above

With your objectives in mind, carefully scrutinize the program. This serves two purposes. You will be able to familiarize yourself with the "names." Then if you should happen to run into one of these people you can say, "Oh, didn't I see your name on the program?" They'll love it. You may even want to make a "to meet" list so you will remember to make a specific effort to meet certain people. It may not seem necessary when you're sitting in the comfort of your living room, but it can become confusing at a conference and you might miss someone.

Second, you can plan your schedule around the sessions that promise to have the greatest benefits for you. You should try to attend all plenary sessions and all social functions. Even if the banquet is overpriced, you should attend to see and be seen. The basic difference between attending a conference and reading books and articles on the same subjects is that you get to meet people and you get to participate. Remember that as you select sessions. Attend those sessions where you will have something to contribute. That means asking a question, making a comment, or cornering someone in the hall before or after the session to start a conversation.

Check to see if the sessions will be tape recorded or available in printed proceedings form. With the increasingly sophisticated audio equipment, more conference planners are contracting with firms that record and distribute cassette tapes right on the spot. You could bring along a pocket tape player and listen to the sessions on the flight home. These factors will affect your scheduling. You can skip those sessions in which you do not expect to take an active part and spend that time meeting people.

One of Your Objectives Is to Meet People, and a Sidekick Is a Serious Interference.

If someone else from your office will be attending the conference, you should have a frank discussion before you get there. One of your objectives is to meet people, and a sidekick is a serious interference. A person who barely talks to you in the office will suddenly cling to you like a rash. Any couple is much less approachable than a single person, so others will avoid both of you. You'll end up accepting or rejecting invitations for meals or drinks based on whether your sidekick is invited, too. You will be talking with someone and then break it off prematurely because you are supposed to meet your sidekick by the drinking fountain as the clock strikes ten.

Most of the time these would-be sidekicks are sorely lacking in self-confidence. Leaning on you won't help them to grow. Do them a favor by kicking them out to fend for themselves. Sometimes they are just being friendly or have a misguided sense of protectiveness. Help them to understand that you appreciate their concerns, but are able to take care of yourself.

You might as well explain up front that you do not wish it to be interpreted as being unfriendly, but that you expect to go off on your own. A nice way to slide into this is to start with the conference schedule and to point out the simple truth that you can cover more sessions if the two of you split up. Even if you end up rooming together, you should each be free to come and go as you please.

Meeting people at a conference is one thing, but the real value lies in building networks of contacts and in becoming a contact for someone else. If you have been to a meeting of this group before, try to think of people you met there. If it would be worthwhile to see them again, call or write to them and try to set up a time. Serious conference-goers may have all of their breakfast, lunch, and dinner partners set up weeks before the conference. They aren't going to leave it to chance encounters at a cocktail party.

If you don't have this information from a previous conference, make sure that you will have it in the future. That means remembering who you met and allowing others to remember that they have met you. The mechanism that has been developed over the years to serve this purpose is the business card.

Every woman who intends to develop any professional image must have a business card. A business card is simply a portable status indicator. You can't take your office or your door plaque with you, but you can carry your business card. A business card says "I am important enough that you will want to remember me." Here are some suggestions regarding business cards:

- Have your own! If your firm does not supply cards, buy them for yourself. A thousand cards will cost less than a tank of gas.
- Keep it simple. Your name, address, title, and phone

number are sufficient. A company logo is fine. Cutesy pictures are out.
- Stick to the standard size and standard colors.
- The higher the quality the better.
- Keep them handy in a pocket or special spot in your briefcase. Don't be caught fumbling.
- Don't be shy. Offer your card with an assertive comment such as "Here is my card." Never ask someone, "Would you like my card?"
- Give your card to anyone you meet in a business setting or to anyone who gives you a card. It's an investment in future business. Remember, a woman is often assumed to be status-less.
- Insert your card when mailing a business letter.
- The only thing you should ever write on your card is a short note such as "Sorry I missed you." Never write in your name or your new address. Keep your card up-to-date and discard old cards.
- When you receive a card, take a moment to study it and make a relevant comment such as "So your office is on Main Street."
- At the end of the day make a few notes on the business cards you have received. You might note the occasion or spouse's name for example. Then file them in your business card file. They will be useful later.

Productive Conference Behaviors

At any conference there are the people who move in the main stream and those who hold up the walls. You can do some things to move closer to the center of the stream of activities. Some of these things take courage, but the majority of them are really just mechanics.

Name Tags Always wear your name tag. This goes for celebrities as much as for everybody else. When a celebrity fails to wear a name tag, it seems to say, "I am so much more important than the rest of you that I don't have to wear this. You should know my name." And everybody else should give other people a chance to get to know them. Why make it difficult? There are lots of excuses: "I don't like to stick pins in my clothes." "Oh, I can never remember it." "It makes me feel foolish." In fact, it is both convenient and courteous. Luvain Bue, a Dale Carnegie Regional Manager and past President of Sales and Marketing Executives of San Francisco, suggests that you wear your name tag on your right lapel. Then people can refer to it easily as you shake hands.

It usually pays to personalize your name tag. For one thing, it gives people an excuse to look at it in case they have forgotten your name or never knew it. People are often embarrassed to glance at your name tag for fear they should know you and you will be offended if they can't recall your name. If you scratch out Pamela and write PAM in big letters, it gives them an excuse. Besides, the people who are too vain to wear their glasses have a better chance. An even better trick is to bring a sticker that represents something about you. A woman from Hawaii always brings a pineapple sticker to represent her state. She gets a lot of attention.

Go to a local stationery supply store and look for something appropriate. You may even share your find. Cheri Marshall got a supply of stickers with phrases like, "SCHZAMM" and "WINNER." She good-naturedly stuck them on other people's name tags. It was as if she had created an instant affiliation group and fan club combined. When the stickered people were asked, "Where did you get that?" they cheerfully answered, "From Cheri Marshall. The tall blonde woman in the navy blazer." People were seeking Cheri out to get a sticker of their own.

If you attend a lot of meetings, you may want to invest in a permanent nametag and wear it even when others don't have one. The brass ones worn by hotel and airline employees are available for individuals. As a speaker, I am always at meetings. I have a special flap of the suiting fabric sewn inside the breast pocket of all my suits. When needed, I flip it out and pin on my personalized petitpoint nametag, which is patterned after my business card.

Approach Behavior Conventions are a collection of people in various states of knowing one another. All of them came to the convention in hopes of meeting some new people and renewing friendships with people from previous conventions. Otherwise they would have stayed home. Now the average conventions lasts about three days. That doesn't give you time for the normal "getting to know someone" routines. But it gives you a reason to practice one of the most productive of all conference activities: approaching people.

Why do we need ice-breakers such as snowball dances at social functions? Without them, a crowd of people might just stand there looking at the floor. You might not believe this, but most people have been taught to be afraid of other people. Most people look at the downside risk. "Unless I am guaranteed a return, I'm not going to play. If I say something to this other person, I might be rebuffed so I will just stand here and pretend that I am all alone." People will stand in line waiting for something, say to buy a ticket. They will stand there in the company of other human beings, yet pretend that they are all alone. Some people take coast-to-coast flights without speaking to their seatmate.

Have our experiences in life been so unpleasant? Maybe it comes from the early childhood admonitions, "Don't say anything until spoken to," or "Don't speak to strangers!" Continuously ask yourself the most important question, *"What is the worst thing that can happen?"* The worst thing is that someone is going to ignore you or even, heaven forbid, be rude. *Sneak off, creep.* So big deal. If you act in a courteous, sincere manner and someone else is rude to you, that's his or her problem, not yours. Most people are lonely and really wish that someone else would break the ice.

Will Rogers used to say, "There are no strangers, only friends I haven't met." Need proof? Look at what happens in crisis. In the recent tornados in Texas, one man was left with nothing but a case of Scotch. What did he do? He invited all of the neighbors to his ruins for a party. The crisis drew them together, but they might have enjoyed the same interaction much sooner.

In a recent survey, a man approached people on the street and asked if they would like to be hugged. Almost 80 percent said yes. If you go up to someone and act as if that person is already or should be your friend, you will find that most people, perhaps 80 percent, respond according to the role you have assigned to them. Isn't that 20 percent lost worth the 80 percent won? Any batter in the major leagues would be thrilled to have an 800 batting average.

And your odds at a conference are even better. Most people at a conference want to talk. Otherwise, they would have stayed home. But the majority of them will stand around waiting for someone else to take the risk of starting the conversation. They are afraid that they will be rejected. The next time you're at a dinner meeting, listen when the people introduce themselves. All of the people from one company will be sitting together. They've been together all day and they may not even like each other, but they'll sit together out of fear of the unknown.

You can assume the responsibility for making the approaches and you can make a lot of valuable friends and contacts in the process. I was once speaking at a meeting where a man approached me with the comment, "I've been thinking all day about how lucky you would be to meet me." I stuck around at least long enough to hear his follow-up line.

Tour the Meeting Facilities and Select a High Traffic Point.

Make the effort to approach people. Tour the meeting facilities and select a high traffic point. It may be the elevator lobby or the exhibit hall entrance. The corridor leading *from* the restrooms is another choice spot. Select a place where people are standing up. It's much harder to approach people at tables. Greet people by name if you can see their name tags. Call them by their first names, just as if you already know them. "Hi Maryann. How are things going?" Maryann won't be sure whether you know her or not. Be sure to shake hands. Most of the time, the person will carry on a brief conversation with you and then hurry off to ask someone else who you are. The next time you meet, she will be the one acting as if you are old friends.

Don't be afraid to approach "celebrities." It can be lonely being a celebrity. Everyone assumes that the celebrity's time is too important to be wasted talking to them and then these poor people end up with no one to talk to at all. Walk right up and introduce yourself to the officers of the association or to the speakers. Ask questions. Show concern for the organization or for the topic. They love the feedback.

Remembering Names Once you have met someone, make the effort to remember that person's name. If you can remember someone's name, you can carry the approach process one step further by introducing that person to someone else. Then you have two people who are grateful to you because you have relieved them of the responsibilities of approaching people. You made it easy for them.

Remembering someone's name is one of the most easily accepted compliments. You've heard every excuse for failing to do so. "I'm great with faces, but I just can't remember names." People love to hear their own names. You may be in a crowded department store and above the din you can hear, "Ms. You, please return to the shoe department." If you pick up a directory or a roster, your eye automatically seeks out your own listing. We all appreciate it when someone, by their actions says to us, "Meeting you was significant enough that I bothered to remember your name." Great! In a few days you might meet 200 new people. How are you going to remember their names?

No one can guarantee immediate success, but here are some ways to get started. First, make sure that you hear the name clearly in the first place. You can't remember something you never knew. It's amazing, but people are reluctant to ask others to repeat their names. Ask! They love it. If you have to, ask them to spell it. So what if she says M-A-R-Y S-M-I-T-H. Then, of course, it helps to repeat the name out loud. "Well, Mary Smith, it's nice to meet you."

It's neat if you can make an association with the name. That is just fine if the person has a colorful name such as Wingwalker, but there are a lot of names where no association comes to mind. The best suggestion is to repeat the person's name three times during your conversation. One way to do this is to be the person to speak up and introduce people as they join your conversation group. But make the effort to remember. Don't cop out with the excuse that you just can't remember names.

Give other people the chance to remember your name. Some people have it easy. Diane Byrd says, "Byrd, but I can't fly." My routine is, "Nope, not Fletcher, *Pletcher*. That's just like Fletcher but with a *P*. *P* as in Peter, P-L-E-T-C-H-E-R. I have a friend who has the difficult name of Kozachok. His routine is "Kozachok. Just like artichoke but it's Kozachok." It works every time.

You want people to remember you, so practice your self introduction. Be phonetic, funny, relevant, or whatever. "Ford— just like the car." "Miller—but unfortunately my dad wasn't into writing plays." "Kinnison—sounds like unison." "Lamar—the French version of a scratch on your tabletop." There are few names which can't be helped along with a little creativity. Always introduce yourself. People are so embarrassed when they can't remember your name. Even people who should know you well can forget your name temporarily. It's so easy to say your own name and relieve that tension.

A Good Handshake   Shake hands as you introduce yourself. One of the most pervasive of all social behaviors is the handshake. While you may not soar to success simply on the basis of your handshake, the lack of handshake consciousness can certainly hold you back. A handshake is like dandruff: No one will tell you if you have a problem, but they will all notice.

A Handshake Is Like Dandruff: No One Will Tell You if You Have a Problem, but They Will All Notice.

A handshake conveys a message of goodwill. By shaking hands you presume some reasonable relationship to other people. You have approached and actually touched them rather than cowering or kneeling in their presence. In general, a well delivered handshake enhances your image. What is a well delivered handshake? Here are some important rules on shaking hands:

Shake hands when you:

- Introduce yourself or when you are introduced
- Reestablish contact, such as calling on a customer
- Greet persons from your firm with whom you do not regularly work
- Encounter co-workers in other settings such as a restaurant
- Reach a verbal agreement with anyone
- End a business encounter
- End a conversation that lasted beyond social amenities

Be prepared to shake hands. Be careful to:

- Carry your briefcase in you left hand
- Keep your hand warm; carry your drink in your left hand
- Keep rings off your right hand; who wants to shake metal?

When you are shaking hands:

- Always stand; never reach up.
- Extend your hand with confidence to both men and women
- Keep your fingers parallel to the floor
- Seek to press the base of your thumb against the base of your partner's thumb and grasp palms not fingers
- Try to exert the same squeeze pressure as your partner
- Actually give a two to six inch shake
- Smile all the while

Be Positive and Supportive Some people are never satisfied. In some misguided way they seem to think they can impress others by criticizing and complaining. The rooms are too warm. The sessions are too long. The coffee is too cold. The meals aren't up to their gourmet standards. It goes on and on. With a little luck these people find each other and leave the rest of us alone. It's interesting that these people seldom complain in constructive sense or to anyone who might be able to do anything about the problem. Complaining is usually an attempt to get attention, but it's the wrong kind of attention.

Complaining Is Usually an Attempt to Get Attention, but It's the Wrong Kind of Attention.

There is always something good to be said. You will attract more people and make stronger contacts if you can emphasize the good in the situation. Instead of broadcasting the one point on which you and the speaker do not agree, think of the three points you found worthwhile. If you are positive and supportive of the efforts of others and the organization, you will attract the doers. You will be in a better position to make a contribution.

Another way to be supportive is to spend some of your time on the nonsessions related to the conference. If there is an exhibit area, be sure to schedule some time to take a look around. You may learn something. And you will be supporting your organization. Exhibitors offset your costs. It is because they pay for exhibit space that the association is able to put on the conference. Few associations prosper because of your registration fees. You are being subsidized by the vendors. The association has, in effect, promised the vendors that a certain number of interested people will pass through their exhibits. You will meet some interesting people, both among the vendors themselves and the people talking with the vendors.

Conference Patterns

All conferences follow a standard pattern. The most common is a beginning and ending half-day with two days of conference in between. One the first half-day, everyone arrives and people mill around seeking affiliations. It's a sort of grouping ritual. Your satisfaction with the conference will depend a lot on your success in this grouping process. Don't be too hasty. Stay away from the negative thinkers. You can recognize them because they have already begun to complain about their flights or the registration lines. Learn to disassociate yourself from people who are hanging on to you. You don't need an excuse to get away from a stranger. You don't owe him or her anything. Simply say, "Would you excuse me please?" and start walking. Search for doers. Look for people with a positive attitude. The best way to attract positive people is to be a positive person yourself.

The Best Way to Attract Positive People Is to Be a Positive Person Yourself.

Ira Hayes always asks his audience, "HOW ARE YOU TODAY?" and they always answer "GREAT!" The world will reflect your attitudes back on you. Everybody remembers the winners. We remember Bruce Jenner, Mohammed Ali, Wilma Rudolph, and many others. We remember them because they are the winners. Do you remember who managed to total up the most strike-outs in professional baseball? It was Babe Ruth. Clearly, he was a bat swinger. He swung the bat more often. That tells us a little bit about how all of these people got to be winners. Some people stand there hoping to walk to first base. Winners keep swinging their bats. They keep at it when others quit.

Don't Be Afraid to Show Enthusiasm.

Don't be afraid to show enthusiasm. It's contagious. Rodney Dangerfield may be able to carry off his "I don't get no respect" act on the nightclub circuit, but that act wears thin elsewhere. If you go through this grouping ritual with a positive attitude and a dose of enthusiasm, you will attract people who, like yourself, are determined to make the most of the experience.

The two full days in between are the time to do most of your work. Morning sessions are usually well attended and then things dwindle off as time passes. So conference planners often put some of the better speakers on in the afternoon to try to smooth out the crowds. Pick your sessions carefully and pace yourself.

Most conferences include cocktail parties sponsored by vendors or special interest groups. These can be important sources of contacts. It is also the place where everyone seeks out dinner companions. Some people seek too hard. Be aware that vendors often scoff at hangers-on who stick around hoping for a free dinner. If a vendor is going to ask you to join in on a dinner party, it will happen within 30 minutes of your arrival.

A young man named Fred was once so persistent in hanging around looking for that elusive free dinner that the vendor was afraid of being late for his dinner reservations. He had already selected his five dinner companions. Finally Fred made the mistake of going into the bathroom. The vendor quickly rounded up his group and herded them out of the suite. Fred was left to wonder what happened.

The third day of a conference is usually the least productive. Everybody is leaving. That creates another problem. Everyone is trying to check out at once. You can beat that problem by checking out the night before. Explain that you want to pay the bill including the night to come and that you don't expect any additional charges.

Nonproductive Conference Behaviors

It's really to your advantage that you go to meetings in dismal places. Then none of your family members will want to go. They will sit at home and feel sorry for you while you get things done. And besides, the hotel rates are always lower. If the meeting is in one of the fun places like Miami Beach, Los Angeles, San Francisco, or the Rockies during ski season, you may end up serving as part-time tour guide. This really tears at you. You have divided loyalties. You are supposed to be attending a luncheon, but when it runs a little late you get indigestion because you know your family members are pacing around in the hotel room anxious to get to Disneyland. You want to strengthen your contacts or share some experiences with some people who you met at a cocktail party, but your spouse has made dinner reservations for two. You lose your flexibility.

It is even worse for women than it is for the man who brings his wife and children to a meeting. Spousal programs are usually oriented toward traditional woman activities such as shopping. And many husbands lack the self-confidence to join a bus load of wives even if the trip would be of interest. Very few programs make any provision whatsoever for children. Having your family around can really strain your professional image.

I took my son, David, to a Data Processing Management Association international conference in Washington, D.C. As I dressed him in his navy blue suit, blue shirt, striped tie, navy socks, and black leather shoes, I explained to him that this was a real threat to my professional image. At seven years of age, he nodded knowingly. I went on to suggest that we would pretend that he was just a small adult. However, he wasn't to do anything without my approval. I left him at the conference headquarters while I presented a session. When I returned, one of the conference coordinators reported that he had refused an ice cream cone because "My mom didn't say I could have it." While his behavior was exemplary and our tourist activities are delightful memories, the stress factor was incredible. If at all possible, have your family join you for two or three days before or after the conference.

You have to get your objectives clearly in mind. Some people do view conventions as tax deductible vacations. If that is your objective, sign up for the tour and see the sights. But if you are there for professional development and advancement, skip the tour bus. Recognize that you only have about 72 hours minus 30 hours maintenance and sleeping time to do your work. These hours are too precious for sights. The only exception is if the people with whom you wish to interact are going on the tour or if the tour is an integral part of the convention schedule.

There aren't many women teaching in the business schools of U. S. universities. Those who are there have both opportunities and responsibilities to advance professionally. There were only seven women among the hundreds of professors registered at the 1976 meeting of the American Marketing Association in Memphis. It was really depressing to hear three of these women discussing their plans to rent a car and go sightseeing for the day. A fourth woman later confided that between sessions and during the meal breaks, she returned to her room to crochet. That's no way to get ahead.

When you consider transportation, lodging, and meal costs, your hourly rate to be at a conference is really high. Beyond that, you have committed yourself to providing some return to your organization. You should be making the most of it and that isn't going to happen if you stay in your room or cower in a corner. Make up your mind that you will develop patterns that will allow you to gain the educational benefits of the conference along with the personal benefits. These professional experiences can be important stepping stones on your career path.

Chapter 10
The People You Leave Behind

Right this very minute millions of gallons of water are cascading over Niagara Falls. Just because you and I aren't there to see it doesn't mean it isn't happening. When you are away from home, life goes on. The big question is, what can you do so that the quality of life doesn't deteriorate?

You may have a number of people with whom you maintain significant relationships. There are husbands, children, roommates, live-ins, parents, and others. Of all of them, children seem to cause the greatest concern.

Your Children

I am frequently asked, "But what about your son?" Sometimes the questioner is only curious. More often it's a plea for help in a similar situation. Once in a while the person's intention is to put me on the spot—to make me feel guilty as a neglectful parent. But, to paraphrase Eleanore Roosevelt, no one can make you feel guilty without your consent.

No One Can Make You Feel Guilty Without Your Consent.

It is a serious question. What *do* you do about your children? If your travel is limited to a few days a year, you don't really have to do anything. You both deserve a vacation from each other. You'll appreciate each other more when you get back together. You can even hope they miss you a lot without feeling guilty. But if your travel is more constant, you should be trying to help your children to adjust in healthy ways. And they *can* adjust. I was once on the road for five weeks straight. At the next parent-teacher conference, my son's third-grade teacher said, "I was absolutely amazed at how easily David accepted your absence." While in a selfish way I wanted to be missed a bit more, I was pleased that some of my efforts had paid off.

Handling Children Before Your Trip First, give your children plenty of warning. Tell them as soon as you know you are going on a trip. Don't spring it on them the night before you leave. It's not like discussions on sex where you are wise to wait and only answer your children's questions as they arise. This is going to happen whether your children are prepared or not. Always tell your children how important it is that you go, and be sure to tell them you are going to enjoy it.

Many women try to cover their feelings of guilt with statements like, "I wish I didn't have to go, but my boss says I have to do it. I'll probably have a miserable time." This causes problems in two ways. First, it casts your boss in the role of the villain and makes you look weak. But more importantly, it confuses your children. "Let's see now. She doesn't want to go on this trip and she thinks she won't enjoy it, but she is going anyway. She must really want to get away from me."

Rather than making your children feel better, negative comments about your travel puts them in the position of being second best to a bad thing. If you emphasize the positive, they are at least only second best to a good thing. "I'm going to get a lot done on this trip and I'm going to have a good time while I'm doing it. I sure am going to be anxious to get home though, cause I miss you a lot. Even when I'm having a good time someplace, I still miss you."

Tell them as much as you can about the place you are going and the people you expect to see there. Give them names to work with. "Remember I told you about Jack Jennings, the guy who works in New York and likes airplane races? I think he's going to be there. And Lynn Schaper should be there, too. I understand she's changed jobs since the last time I saw her." The idea is to color in the picture for your children—to give them thoughts to hold onto while you're gone.

Let them participate in the planning process. You might even ask for their opinions. "Do you think I should stay at the Holiday Inn or the Ramada Inn?" And be prepared to act according to your children's opinion. One of the problems children face with traveling parents is that the parent moves beyond the child's sphere of experiences and outside of the child's control. By allowing your children to share in those experiences with solid details and to participate in the decision making, you have relieved some of those feelings of inadequacy.

Tell Your Children What You Are Going to Be Doing and How It Fits With the Daily Schedule at Home.

Get out a map and show your children where you are headed. Katie's mother travels extensively and Katie takes pride in her wall-mounted map with colored map pins stuck in the places her mother has been. Talk about your routine while you are on the road. Tell your children what you are going to be doing and how it fits with the daily schedule at home. "Just about the time you are getting on the schoolbus, I am usually going into my first meeting."

Try to get your children to talk about their fears and feelings. It's much better to bring these out in the open and deal with them than to let them smolder in their little heads. A good way to start is by suggesting a mild fear. "Do you ever wonder if I'll get lost when I'm traveling?" Your children might say yes or no, but the point you are communicating is that it is alright to have fears, that you expect your children to have fears and that you want to talk about them.

Children usually feel guilty about the feelings they have about their parents' careers and travel—whether it is the father or the mother. My son confessed to me that he sometimes wished the place where I was scheduled to go would burn down—before I got there, of course. He reasoned that that would mean that I would cancel my trip.

The kinds of fears your children have change as they grow older. A small child is simply afraid that you won't come back or that you'll get hurt. Maybe they think they can protect you better at home. An older child may have friends whose parents are divorced and be afraid that you will decide you'd rather live someplace else. Some of your children's fears are legitimate. Others can be soothed away easily. If your children are afraid that you won't be able to get back in case there is an emergency, you can explain that you are constantly available by phone and would cancel your plans and be home within hours. Even though some of the things you hear will make you feel badly, you will be better off to deal with your children's concerns before they are blown out of proportion.

Children need attention. If they aren't helped to deal with their fears and frustrations in constructive ways, they will find other ways to get that attention. This can turn into a battleground and breed guilt and frustration in both the parents and the child. One solution is good attention/bad attention. Even a preschool child can understand the concept. Make a deal with your children and stick with it. "I will give you attention when you need it. All you have to do is ask. Don't put the cat in the dryer or pour mustard on the floor. Come and ask for attention. Tell me what is bothering you. It's alright. I will stop what I'm doing and give you the attention you deserve. Your feelings are important to me." About four minutes of direct honest undivided attention is usually all it takes.

If Your Work and Your Travels Are Mysteries to Them, They Tend to Imagine the Worst.

If at all possible, arrange to bring your children, one at a time, on one business trip—even if only to a nearby town. Let them see what you do. My mother is a retired educator. When I was in grade school, I spent many hours grading the objective tests for her high school courses. As children understand more about your work and your activities, it becomes easier to accept that part of your life as a part of their lives. If your work and your travels are mysteries to them, they tend to imagine the worst. As far as they are concerned, you have fallen off the edge of the earth.

During the Trip Small children are a lot like dogs. Their perception of time isn't very good. When you leave they wonder if you will ever come back. Give them some mechanism to count the days. As soon as they can read you can leave them a note to open each day you will be gone. If it is a long trip, you can mail them letters. Kids love to get mail. Linda makes three-day trips about twice a month. She has worked out an interesting mechanism for her preschooler to keep track of the days. The child always has cereal for breakfast. Before she leaves she sets out cereal bowls for each day she will be gone. He knows that his mother will be home as soon as all of the bowls are used up. When he gets older, Linda plans to switch over to a paper bag a day with a craft project or game in each. Psychological researchers have shown that people can stand just about anything if they know when it is going to end. It's the uncertainty that gets to them. Try to think of things that will relieve the uncertainty and your children will be better able to adjust to your absence.

You can make some effort to make your presence felt even if you aren't there. Kathy has taped a picture of herself and a sign "Momma loves you!" on the bottom of the upper bunk of her daughter's bed. She sleeps on the lower bunk and sees her mother's picture when she goes to bed. It can't hurt.

Be sure to call home often. Its sounds simple, but it isn't. You can be caught up in the events of a convention and suddenly realize that you haven't called home for three days. Time zones can be a hassle. You might be free to call home in the morning, but if you're east the they're west, it might be 5:00 AM. You'll probably find them all in, but they won't be happy with you. Regardless of the timing, don't be discouraged if your children don't have much to say to you. They seem to be quite satisfied to say "Hi" and then be off to play ball. All they really want is to know that you still exist. But that can be hard on you. You're the one who is all alone and far away. They are still there in the comfort and security of their home sleeping in their own beds. Even if the phone calls aren't satisfying to you, remember that they are doing some good.

After the Trip When you first start to travel, you may be tempted to arrive home with gifts. It is a fairly widespread practice for pleasure travelers. And it may help to relieve your guilt feelings—temporarily. But be careful. Just think of the bears at Yellowstone Park. Every summer the story is the same. Some tourist starts to feed cookies to the bears. The bears stand on their hind legs and do little tricks for the camera snappers. But when the bag is empty, the bears don't understand. The tourist is lucky to escape in one piece. People are only slightly more sophisticated animals. You must never start anyone off on a diet of rewards that you cannot maintain.

You Must Never Start Anyone Off on a Diet of Rewards That You Cannot Maintain.

So it's really best to avoid bringing gifts, especially costly gifts. Your children should be happy that you are home and will sense it if you try to buy off your guilt feelings with a present. It can be quite a blow to arrive home some day without a gift and find that you aren't quite welcome. Once it gets started, the gift giving routine tends to escalate. If a $5.00 gift was good enough the first time, it takes $10.00 to buy your enthusiastic reception the next time.

If you do bring gifts, try to establish some routine that involves both you and your children and becomes part of your travel preparation routine. One woman who sells college text books is building a collection of campus seal paperweights with her child. They are fairly inexpensive, easily stored, and provide for a sense of shared purpose. Another woman always brings home a piece of stationery found in the desk drawer at the hotel. She is especially pleased with the hotels that provide picture postcards.

There are lots of possibilities. Hopefully your children won't become so involved that they start to ask you to go on trips. My son feeds me that line whenever my culinary experiments turn out badly. Matchbook collections are another choice. Make it something that won't become a burden to you. I once wanted a set of American Airline wings for my son's collection. They didn't have any on the plane, so Captain Charles Sweet went down to the flight crew quarters to see if he could find some. When he came back empty handed, he asked for my business card and later sent the wings to my son along with a personal note. Just imagine what that did for my status at home.

While you're traveling your adrenalin is up. It can be a natural high. At a meeting or convention you may find yourself going almost around the clock. When you hit home all of the fatigue hits you like a giant club. Now that you are home safely, you can relax. Lots of times I can hardly stay awake in the car for the 20 minutes it takes to get home from the airport. I'm just a bundle of fun! But force yourself. Talk about your trip. Tell them about the people you saw. The temptation is to bring home the stories of the difficulties and aggravations of travel. Be careful to balance those with stories of pleasant moments. As one little girl put it, "My dad always talks about the terrible drivers and bad things that happen during the day while my mom tells tells me about the funny people and the things she gets done. I like that better." Share the purpose and the excitement of your trip with your family and the pain of separation will be lessened.

Husbands and Lovers

It's tough enough to be the husband of a professional woman, and tougher yet to be the mate of a traveling professional woman. It can bring on some real burdens. First, when you're traveling, you aren't there to assume even a fair share of the normal household responsibilities. Second, some people aren't quite ready to accept the idea of a women traveling alone and can take a lot of cruel shots at your husband: "Where's Barbara this week?" (snear and snicker).

Woman's Work Remember the story about the farm couple who switched roles? She went out to the fields and he stayed home to tend the child and the house. By the end of the day she had finished plowing the field, but he ended up with an overturned churn, a cow stuck on the roof, and general chaos. The moral of the story may be

1. Women are more adaptable than men;
2. The grass is always greener; or
3. We have our assigned responsibilities and should stick to them.

But think about how we divide common and necessary household responsibilities. It may be on the basis of tradition. If both your mother and his mother kept the household books, you may well end up with the task. It may be on the basis of convenience. If you get home a half-hour earlier and he drives past the dry cleaners, you may end up cooking dinner while he picks up the cleaning. But then if you move and he doesn't have to drive so far to work, do the chores change hands?

Your Guilt and Frustration Level Will Be Inversely Related to Your Family Members' Abilities to Fend for Themselves.

Your guilt and frustration level will be inversely related to your family members' abilities to fend for themselves. Some women do all of the laundry, grocery shopping, and cleaning before they head for the airport. There is probably some ego satisfaction in this behavior. You can say to yourself, "They really couldn't get along without me."

But there are really two kinds of work in any household. There are the responsibilities that continue on a regular basis and there are the special projects. Watering the plants is a continuing responsibility. Left in my care, plants die. Filing the income tax return is a special project. The trick to the division of labor in a traveler's household is to assign the traveler to the special projects and the nontraveler to the continuing projects. If neither of you is a nontraveler, don't buy any plants and hire someone to do the rest of it.

If you travel a lot, you must realize that you abdicate your authority in the home. I once returned from a trip and my husband informed me that he had set it up for our house to be painted. He pulled out a paint chip card and pointed to the most awful park bench green. "How do you like it?" I swallowed hard and answered, "Looks fine." If you're not there to vote, you have no right to criticize the outcome of the election. He laughed and pointed to the color he had really selected, a respectable California earth-tone. He knows that I know that responsibility and authority must go hand in hand. If I expect him to "hold down the fort," I have to be willing to live with the decisions he makes in my absence.

Sometimes Those Decisions Can Tear at Your Sense of Values.

Sometimes those decisions can tear at your sense of values. If you are traveling, you must abdicate the right to make some of the decisions relative to your children. Someone is deciding what they will eat and when they will go to bed. Someone will decide if they are sick enough to be taken to the doctor. If you're not there, there is only so much you can say. Ginger Marquart, a purchasing agent, says that her youngest child confided that discipline relaxes in her absence. "We didn't make our beds all week. And I got to stay up late last night because we had a lot of cleaning to do before you came home. Don't tell Dad I told you."

There have been stories of widowers who can't find their way to the grocery store or turn on the washing machine. Start your husband and children off right. Don't do all of the work before you leave home. Give guidance. If they get hungry, they'll eat.

If you are traveling, you are undoubtedly more upwardly mobile than someone who isn't traveling. Therefore, in the long run, you can avoid some of the drudgery. In the short run, you should quickly volunteer for some of the special projects to balance off the other burdens that are placed on your mate. By the way, that same strategy works for responsibilities outside the home. Call up the people at the PTA, the Little League, the church, or civic group and volunteer for times or projects that don't conflict with your travel schedule. Don't wait until they call you. Get those responsibilities out of the way early. "I will be in town most of the month of April. Could I help out then?" "I won't be in town on the day of the school fair, but I'd be happy to work on the publicity or another committee that does its work before the day of the fair."

These matters are far less important than the emotional factors that crop up due to separation. Some people drive each other crazy and need a break now and then, but a steady travel diet brings pressures on any relationship.

Snicker, Snicker One of the biggest pressures is the outside detractor. This might be the one who invites your "poor husband" to dinner. The underlying message is that he is being neglected. It's the nurd at the office who winks at your husband and implies that "the cat's away so it's time for the mouse to play." It's the relative who consoles you and your husband on your occasional separation.

Left alone, the two of you could get along just fine. But why are so few people willing to let other people lead their own lives? When a man travels, it is quite acceptable. His wife is supposed to accept it. She is supposed to adjust. She is supposed to care for her home and children and be pleased that her husband is moving up in the world. No one questions his ability to meet his household, parental, or conjugal responsibilities. When women travel, the double standard thrives. Your husband's friends may run through all of the tacky one liners:

- That's okay. We'll fix you up with hot and cold running maids.

- Say, have your seen your wife lately?
- Do you still remember what she looks like, or better yet (snicker snicker), what she feels like?
- Oh boy, bet she's having a great time. She always was a livewire.

Between the pity and the potshots, your husband doesn't have much of a chance. It takes a very strong person to withstand the continuous pressure. Now that we understand the problem, what can be done about it? It's probably too late to suggest that you marry a particularly strong and patient man. Well, the next best thing is to recognize the pressures and help your husband build up his defenses. Your husband needs to know that you appreciate his support and that you realize that some people can't understand your unique relationship. He needs to know that your travel is an integral part of your career, that's it's not just a reason to escape. He needs to know about your accomplishments so that he can answer with pride and confidence when some petty meddler questions him, "Well, why does she have to go to Washington for so long?" "She has gone to Washington to . . . ."

You can work together to build up these defenses against the outside detractors. It requires sharing. There are many ways to share. If you call home and relate some interesting incident or give an up-date on your accomplishments, your husband has an answer for that "Where's your wife this week?"

There is a great sense of security in a relationship where each partner enjoys the other's company yet knows that the other one can survive and surmount obstacles individually. Each person grows stronger.

You see, you can have a great control over your life. That's the essence of travel savvy. It is realizing that you are responsible for yourself. With some thought, some planning, and some courage, you can substantially improve your situation. You can take actions to assure that you will be more effective, more comfortable, happier, and more satisfying to those who are important to you. Have a good trip.

Index

A
Action attitude, 17
Air Transport Association, 45
Airline clubs, 75-6
Airline safety, 71-2
Airline tickets:
   Buying, 61-6
   Lost, 29
   Red eyes, 69
   Special meals, 71
American Airlines, 54, 62
American Express, 129
American Management Association, 151
Amorous clients, 41-3

B
Barrie, Roz, 142
Berton, Denise (*Businesswomen*), 130
Borcover, Al (*Chicago Tribune*), 103, 105, 140, 143
Boylan, Ann, 54, 57, 62, 74
Braniff Airlines, 36, 67
Bruce, Anne (*Women's Advocate*), 99, 119
Bue, Luvain, 162
Bumping, 31
Business cards, 160-1
Business Traveler's Review, 72, 84
Businesswoman, 130
Busses, 78-80

C
Cabs, 77-80
Car trouble, 38

Carte Blanche, 129
Cash, 126-8
Charge cards, 128-30, 143-4
Chicago Tribune, 103
Children, 171-7
Cleary, Ruth, 57
Conferences:
   Importance, 147
   Preparation for, 158-61
   Productive behaviors at, 161-7
   Support for, 151-8
Coffman, DeWitt (*Living Hospitality*), 14

D
Data Processing Management Association, 148-9, 155
Diner's Club, 129

E
Eastern Airlines, 9, 130
Eating Alone, 102-7
Encyclopedia of Associations, 150
Exercise, 137-9
Expense accounts, 130-2

F
Farrell, June, 9, 13
Fears, 12-3
Foxworth, Jo (*Boss Lady*), 150-1
Frontier Airlines, 61

G
Gifts, 175-6
Guaranteed Reservations, 92

H

Handshakes, 165-6
Holiday Inns, Inc., 89, 90
Hotels:
  Check in, 93-96
  Early check out, 100
  Fires, 18-19
  Late check out, 100
  Safety, 96-9
  Selection, 86-91
Housework, 177-9
Husbands, 177-80

I J K

Jenkins, Barbara, 36, 67, 127
Jet lag, 76-7

L

Living Hospitality, 14
Lloyd, Kate (*Working Woman*), 13
Lofft, Virginia (*Successful Meetings*), 91, 94, 147-8
Luggage:
  Checking, 45-8
  Lost, 32-4
  Selecting, 48-53

M

Mastercard, 129
Menu terms, 113
Money clips, 127
Moskal, LilyB, 51, 55, 62
Murphy's Laws of Travel, 14

N

Name tags, 161-2
Names, remembering, 164-6
National Association of Insurance Women, 4
National Association for Professional Saleswomen, 150
National Speaker's Association, 54

O P Q

Obligation Trap, 144-5
Official Airline Guide (OAG), 66, 68-9, 90
Packing list, 54-6
Palmer, Edward, 148
Positive mental attitude, 17
Power of Joint Committment, 22, 35
Power of Silence, 22, 26
Purse snatchers, 31

R

Rental cars, 81-4, 129
Restaurants:
  Checks, 115-6
  Selecting, 9-11
Robert, Cavett, 74

S

Sacramento Bee, 40
Sales and Marketing Executives, 150, 162
Self-determination attitude, 19
Schulman, Bob, 61
Sickness, 37
Lee Smith (*Sacramento Bee*), 40
Socio-feminist stages, 7
Status evaporation, 10
Successful Meetings, 91, 147

T

Telephone, 22-3, 133-4
Tipping:
  Airports, 123
  Cab drivers, 123-4
  Hotels, 124-5
  Restaurants, 126-7
Travel agents, 62-3, 90
Travel wardrobe, 55-6
Traveler's checks, 128
Trip list, 54

U V W X Y Z

Visa, 129
Women's Advocate, 99, 119
Zimrich, Glenys, 155